ONE STEP AHEAD OF HITLER

MERCER
UNIVERSITY PRESS

Endowed by
TOM WATSON BROWN
and
THE WATSON-BROWN FOUNDATION, INC.

ONE STEP AHEAD OF HITLER

A Jewish Child's Journey through France

Fred Gross

MERCER UNIVERSITY PRESS

MACON, GEORGIA

MUP/P420

First Paperback Edition.

Books published by Mercer University Press are printed on acid free paper
that meets the requirements of American National Standard for Information
Sciences—Permanence of Paper for Printed Library Materials.

Mercer University Press is a member of Green Press initiative
(greenpressinitiative.org), a nonprofit organization working to help publishers
and printers increase their use of recycled paper and decrease their use of
fiber derived from endangered forests. This book is printed on recycled paper.

Library of Congress Cataloging-in-Publication Data
Gross, Fred, 1936-
One step ahead of Hitler : a Jewish child's journey through France / Fred
Gross. -- 1st ed.
p. cm.
Includes bibliographical references and index.
SBN-13: 978-0-88146-225-8
1. Gross, Fred, 1936- 2. Jews—Belgium—Antwerp—Biography. 3. Jews,
Belgian—France—Biography. 4. Refugees, Jewish—France—Biography.
5. Jewish children in the Holocaust—France—Biography. 6. Holocaust, Jewish
(1939-1945)—France—Personal narratives. 7. France—Biography. I. Title.
DS135.B43G784 2009
940.53'18092—dc22 [B]
2009007889

In memory of the children lost in the Holocaust

CONTENTS

FOREWORD

It is a great privilege to offer a word of introduction and commendation for Fred Gross and his important memoir, *One Step Ahead of Hitler*, a riveting tale of Holocaust survival that will be among the last to surface as even those who suffered through that era as small children now pass from the earth and into the arms of God.

This is a story of a Jewish family on the run from Hitler's murderous hatred for five long years, from the day the bombs fell in their Antwerp neighborhood on 10 May 1940 until the war ended with Nazi Germany's defeat.

In their desperate quest for survival, the Gross family simply tried to stay "one step ahead of Hitler" in a journey that took them thousands of miles across the length and breadth of France and beyond. Matching wits with a regime determined to annihilate every single Jew it could reach, the Gross family faced agonizing emotional and physical suffering and the torment of decisions as to how best to survive yet one more day.

As Fred Gross tells the story of his family's desperate sojourn across southwestern Europe, those who are familiar with the basic outlines of the events now called the Holocaust gain much greater clarity as to what daily life was like on the run from the Nazis. And the particular trajectory taken by the Gross family leads them into brushes with numerous important figures who are well-known to Holocaust historians. In these pages, for exam-ple, we meet Aristede de Sousa Mendes, the heroic Portuguese diplomat in Bordeaux who defied his government to give out transit visas to Jews, and Varian Fry, sometimes called America's Righteous Gentile, whose actions in Marseille saved thousands of Jewish lives.

In these pages we also encounter not so much individuals as types of characters who are important in the history of the Holocaust. Those on the side of life include the *passeurs* who (for a price) helped Jews cross into Switzerland; the Italian diplomats, representing Germany's key ally but (to Italy's eternal honor) committed to saving rather than killing Jews in Italian-occupied zones; Christian families who for reasons of conscience or faith aided and sheltered Jewish strangers, and Jewish community organizations trying to help Jews survive.

But scoundrels also abound here. The chief scoundrel is Adolf Hitler himself, the hateful tyrant who from the first pages of this memoir is understood to be hunting the Gross family personally in his insane quest for Jewish blood. But there are also lesser scoundrels, including the German military, bombing civilian refugees from the sky in 1940; the French Vichy regime, with its enthusiastic support for and collaboration with the murder of helpless Jews in its territory; the Swiss government, with its closed-door policy toward Jewish refugees and return of captured Jews to the French police or the Gestapo, and thus certain death; and the all-too-easily propagandized French population, like so many others before it, turning on Jews as enemies of the state under the influence of a bit of Vichy government propaganda. Some of the most shameful moments of German, French, Swiss—and human—history are recorded here, not for the first time, but in a deeply personal way by someone who experienced their effects as a small child.

One of the unique virtues of this memoir is in fact the narrative voice of this child. As the story begins, Fred Gross is barely three years old. His memories can only be sketchy. Inevitably, he wants to know more. He will need to consult his family—his mother and two much older brothers. But it seems that no one wants to talk about what happened, that in fact no one really does talk about what happened until Fred Gross begins pressing for answers in the 1980s. By this time his father is dead, his memories taken with him to the grave. The author takes us inside the conversations he has with his mother and older brothers and gives us a glimpse of the painful family dynamics involved in undertaking such conversations.

The author deftly mixes together the perspective of a three-year-old, at the beginning of the war, a child with few memories of his own and almost entirely dependent on the rest of his family for their stories; and then a four-to-eight-year old on the run, with his own dawning memories; and then a fully grown adult, able not only to ask questions of family members but to gather critically important historical information that can help him understand what was happening to his family at each juncture. We watch the author watching his young self going through these traumatic experiences—at each moment the reader somehow experiences the events both through the eyes of a small child and a grown man remembering what it was like to be that small child. The effect is profound.

One final note: those of us who have been blessed with families of our own can only resonate deeply with something else young/old Fred Gross is watching—his family. Fred is trying to understand what his parents went through, the options they faced, the decisions they made, and the kind of relationship they had with each other as they staggered through these terrifying days. He is also watching his oldest brother, Sam, as he is eventually forced to take life-threatening risks to help his family survive. Fred also takes the narrative back into the histories of both sides of his family, a history of Jewish identity constantly marked by persecution and suffering.

It is important to remember this: Hitler attacked not just Jewish individuals but Jewish families. He wanted each Jew dead, but to kill them he would have to destroy them one family at a time. In this story, we watch Fred's parents, Max and Nacha, trying to save the lives of their children, facing impossible choices with limited resources amidst growing exhaustion and constant fear. Aunts and uncles and other relatives appear at critical times, doing what families do—trying to help each other.

In the end, *One Step Ahead of Hitler* offers the very good news that not even Hitler and his murderers could destroy every Jewish family in Europe, and so the Jewish people survived—viciously assaulted, decimated and traumatized, millions murdered, but the people survived. Thanks be to God—and to every person who fought hard for life amidst the Nazi slaughterhouse.

David P. Gushee
Distinguished University
Professor of Christian Ethics,
Mercer University

PREFACE

Once I was just a child living in Belgium with my family, until suddenly Hitler came to my town, and, in many ways, ending my childhood and beginning a remarkable and dangerous journey. Today, I tell my story to people to give a face, a voice to a child of war and the impact that war had on me. Once, after I had just finished telling my story to a class of sixth graders, a student asked me, "Does that come from your memory or did your family tell you all this?"

The student had put me in a tight spot. I wanted to say that it was all my memory because I was afraid that if I told her otherwise, she might feel disappointed. And then there was this nagging question: Would she believe my story? Would anyone, if I wasn't the primary source?

"I was only three years old when it began," I answered, "so I had to rely on my mother and two brothers for much of my memories. My brother Sam was sixteen years old and Leo was eleven. But I remember more from when I was five and six years old."

That remark was a plea for her to pay attention to my story and not to doubt because some of my story was more family memory than personal memory. It was a challenge to redefine memory, and to whom memory belongs, which I presented to her, and to myself in writing this book.

Searching for memories is like rummaging through the attic to find a dust-covered home movie that you haven't watched in decades. When you play it, all you see are faded images, except for a few frames that bring into sharp focus some long-forgotten scenes, letting you know that you haven't forgotten at all. "Can you remember everything that happened to you when you were three years old?" the teacher asked the class. "Of course not, but maybe you can remember one thing, like your favorite toy. That's what Fred is talking about."

This book is about a very young Jewish boy, who waited until 1988—more than forty years—to find out what had happened to him when Nazi Germany destroyed his childhood. My journey into the past began with a conversation with my mother, and her first words of recollection, "I looked out the window and down came this piece from a bomb." It continued through interviews with my two older brothers, and my personal viewings of that blurred home movie that lives in my mind. A Nazi warplane had dropped that bomb. My mother told me of many other events that happened on our journey. Some were unbelievable. Some were horrible. And what she forgot, or chose not to remember, I asked my brothers to recall. I was the reporter; they were my eyes. I was the outsider to my own story; they were helping me to return as a witness, and bringing my movie into focus a frame at a time.

I forced them to remember the roads we traveled, the cities, villages, and farmhouses where we stopped to rest and eat, and I asked for details, details, details. Sometimes my relentless pursuit stirred memories they would have rather forgotten and not ever talked about to anyone. And sometimes they did simply forget. "If I knew you wanted to write a book, I would have kept notes," Leo said years later, half in jest, half in pain.

Still, with all my questioning there were gaps. Then finally all of the details started to come together when I discovered two yellow faded identification cards in my mother's old hat box after she died in 1989. They were stamped with names of French cities and towns, and the dates we went through each as we tried to escape from Hitler's henchmen. The French police required adult foreigners to carry these ID cards or face immediate arrest.

And yet, the information I had gathered from these documents and my family wasn't enough. I needed to see the big picture. I needed to look over my own shoulder to see how close the German troops were when we fled Antwerp. Where were they when we crossed into France? Where were they? I felt as if they were in some ways still pursuing me now. I needed to know how close we came to peril, and to know with exactness. I needed a military account of what was happening in spring 1940, not from history books, but from the very scourge that changed my life: Adolf Hitler.

The most illuminating moment of my research came when I spent an entire day at Fort Knox, Kentucky, the fabled army base less than an hour's drive from Louisville, where I live. My good friend, Dick Thornton, who was then communications director for Fort Knox's school system for children of military personnel, arranged the visit. The base houses a famous depository of more than $6 billion in gold. During World War II, the original copies of the Constitution, Declaration of Independence, Lincoln's "Gettysburg Address," and Magna Carta were placed there for safekeeping. During my research, a helpful librarian handed me something that was far more valuable to me than all the gold in Fort Knox: a huge book, bound in black that had belonged to Adolf Hitler. He had given it as a gift in gratitude to one of his generals leading the assault on Belgium. American troops found it in 1944, after the Allied invasion of Normandy. Inside were Hitler's military maps of his invasion into Belgium. These maps offered a day-to-day account of German movements from 10 May through 20 May 1940. As I turned the pages, I saw arced lines representing German forces that expanded as if someone was blowing air into a balloon, covering all of Belgium. I stared at these pages, tracing the movement of the Nazis, trying to figure out where I had been trapped. The more I stared at the maps, the more they seemed to take on a life of their own. I saw myself running across the pages with Hitler chasing after me.

But it wasn't just a moment of fantasy. It was memory.

Yes, in 1940, danger hung over us like a storm cloud, as the arcs on the map maneuvered south, on our very heels, following us deep into France where most of my adventures took place. That place, France, only raised more questions when I returned there as an adult. Why did the French police send us to a concentration camp in southern France? Why did we have to go into hiding in August 1942? Why was it dangerous to try even to escape from France? Into Spain, into Switzerland? Was any border safe? The answers soared from the pages of books that I found in public libraries and hunted down on the Internet. Documents stored at Holocaust museums in Washington, New York, and Paris were now available to me and they explained the reasons behind the complicated and terrible circumstances of my personal tour of France.

And so, at the end of my writing of this book, and at the beginning of your reading of it, we come back to the young student's question, does this story come from my memory? Does it matter? Yes, it does, because in a way the reign of Hitler was an attempt to separate people and nations from each other and their histories, to erase from history those things that Hitler, in his madness, wished had never existed.

Well, despite his terrible efforts, we continue, and this book is a product of our unity, a product of people and nations who have come together to be family again, and not to forget. This does come from my memory, and from the memory of those he sought to silence, and from the long memory of history. Soon it will come from your memory too, and so we must continue to retell the story, for the sake of those the madness destroyed, those who once were in our family, but who will never be able to tell us what they remember.

ACKNOWLEDGMENTS

Where do I begin? I had labored for many years writing this book, suffered along with many friends who had repeatedly asked, "When is the book coming out?" Still, they steadfastly stood by me with every word that survived the test of time, or was discarded. And I am grateful to them all, reserving my greatest appreciation for Carolyn Humphrey, the guiding force behind this story. The seminal moment came one day in September 1985 on our European honeymoon in Antwerp, Belgium. My oldest brother Sam was in town on business, and the brother between us, Leo, who lived in Paris, joined to share this momentous occasion. It was the first time since May 1940 that all three brothers had been together in the city they left behind.

We went for lunch at a restaurant on the Keyserlei, Antwerp's Fifth Avenue. There, Carolyn gently prodded my brothers to talk a little bit about their war experiences. Sam did most of the talking, revealing things I was hearing for the first time. His words did not flow readily, but Carolyn helped ease the words out for Sam. Leo did the listening, and I could tell he was translating Sam's words into his own vision of what happened. His eyes were off in space.

At first, I listened to Sam as the journalist I was, dispassionate and disengaged. As his journey unfolded and when he reached critical moments that held our lives in balance, it began to flash in my mind, "Wait a minute, this is my story too."

And that's how it all began. Carolyn was the light that opened the then empty pages of my book, and then others came along to help me fill them, especially Vanessa Weeks and Dianne Thomas. Vanessa framed much of the content, advised me on how to fill the gaps, and helped me strengthen my sense of perspective. Dianne nurtured it to maturity, advising me on how to give it a unique personality and to show emotion behind the words, to loosen up the journalistic part that has consumed most of my life.

My cousin, Mortimer Gross, the youngest son of my father's oldest brother Joe, the first to come to America, provided me with much of the rich and turbulent history of the Gross family's ordeal in Germany and Poland years before Hitler romped his way to power. I am grateful for his contribution.

Above all else, I am grateful to my mother and two brothers for opening themselves up, reliving the pain and anguish of their wartime experiences, to fill the void that was my early childhood. Without them, there would be no story to tell. And without my father's streetwise boldness, I would not have existed to tell it.

Father and Freddy, with mother shown adjusting handbag,
during Rosh Hashanah, Jewish New Year, 1938.

Sam, mother, Leo, and Freddy enjoy their annual summer retreat
in Knokke, a seaside resort off the Belgian coast, 1939.

Nacha and Max on beach
in Knokke, 1938.

Camp Gurs, where Gross family and other Jewish refugees were
imprisoned by the French government, starting June 1940.

Leo teaching Freddy how to ride bicycle on grounds of Hôtel Continental, Nice, France, 1941.

Freddy and his first best friend, Mickey Abet, who lived with his mother at Hôtel Continental, 1941.

Sam, 17 years old, May 1941.

Mother, Freddy, and Leo on the Promenade des Anglais, a long walkway that hugs the beach beside the Mediterranean Sea in Nice, July 1942. This is the last photo taken in Nice before the French police begin arresting and deporting thousands of Jews to the death camps in Poland.

Freddy, front, and Leo, back row, right, with youths, in displaced persons camp in Münchwilen, Switzerland, January 1943.

Freddy, left, and his school friends in St. Gallen, Switzerland, fall 1943.

Freddy and Max Maurer, his best friend,
in Zürich, Switzerland,
February 1946.

Last photo taken of Grandmother Rachel
before Leo, left, Max, Freddy, and Nacha
leave for America, February 1946.

Freddy back home in Antwerp,
March 1946.

Freddy on deck of American military freighter docked in Antwerp destined to a new home, April 1946.

Leo, left, Sam, and Fred, in September 1985, reuniting in Antwerp for the first time since fleeing their home. The second floor balcony where young Fred had a few misadventures collapsed from the May 1940 bombings.

Rachel and her teenage daughter
Nacha in Leipzig, Germany,
c. 1916–1917.

Teenager Max was drafted to fight on
the German side during World War I,
1915–1916.

Uncle Emil,
Max's twin brother,
served in the French army
during World War II,
1939.

Max visits his sister Hedwig
in Germany, 1935.

Map of Gross family journey.

HOLLAND

NAZI INVASION
MAY 10, 1940

Antwerp
Leave 5/13/40

BELGIUM
SURRENDER
5/28/1940

: 5-17

LUXEMBOURG

NAZI GERMANY

Return to Antwerp 2/1946

IS:
NTER
40

FRANCE
SURRENDER
6/22/1940

Zurich

Reunited 2/44

St. Gallen 2/3-2/44
Foster Home

AUSTRIA

Münchwilen
Displaced Persons Camp

SWITZERLAND

Escape
Border
Patrol
10/3/42

Geneva

Vichy

HY FRANCE

ITALY

Grenoble

ORS BEGIN JEWISH ROUNDUPS 8/42

ED TO AUSCHWITZ

Nice

Escape
Hotel Raid
8/25/42

Marseille

MEDITERRANEAN SEA

Father's Belgian identification card showing dates of important events during journey in France.

Chapter 1

HITLER INVADES MY HOME

A light film of blue was unfolding in the sky over the city of Antwerp, Belgium, where we had our home, and there was just a pale hint of the sun preparing to break through that Friday, 10 May 1940, when the rumbling sounds of thunder startled us from our sleep. Mama opened the window and saw black clouds of smoke rising from the direction of the thunder, a site not far away from home.

"Max, come here quickly," she called, panicked. Shrapnel whizzed by her, close enough to almost part her hair.

Mama recalled decades later when I interviewed her for the first time about our experiences during the Second World War in October 1988: "I could have been hit," she said, lost in her thoughts as her eyes roamed around the room of her tiny apartment wedged in with others in a high-rise senior citizen housing complex, fixing her gaze at the ceiling, as if waiting for that scorching hot piece of metal to descend toward her. "We really went through something," she uttered with a heavy sigh. "Ya, ya."

Papa rushed to the window, the flimsy white curtains fluttering in the morning breeze, a worried, but not frantic, look on his face. He saw planes swooping down to strafe people on the street running for cover. One of the pilots, Gottfried Leske, reacting to a colleague's reluctance to join in this sport, wrote: "They are our enemies, aren't they? One must kill his enemies!

Who are we to decide whether to do or not to do? The Führer decides."

The bombardments were mainly aimed at military bases and airfields, and these were wiped out in the first wave of attacks.

"Turn on the radio," Father said. He grabbed for his cigar, a custom he usually followed to wake himself up, but this time he bit down hard on it with his yellow-stained teeth rather than rolling it around his lips and enjoying the taste of tobacco.

"It's the Germans," my older brother Sam said softly, listening to the radio. I can remember the sound of the panicky announcer as he blurted out words that made no sense except to my parents and brothers. Germany was attacking; troops were storming across Belgium, Holland, and Luxembourg with tanks and soldiers and motorcycles and guns and rifles and cannons and bombs. And bombs were pounding down on our home of Antwerp.

My parents were hurling a lot of words toward each other. I stared at my two older brothers, Sam and Leo, waiting for them to walk out. That's what they usually did when Mama and Papa engaged in a shouting match. I'd run to the other room and play with my toy train set, or throw myself onto the bed and pound my head on the pillow until exhaustion lulled me to sleep. This time was different; this time my brothers stood frozen, their faces drained of any color, too scared to move.

"What are we going to do?" Mama asked as she quickly dressed me, her fingers nervously fumbling with my shirt buttons.

"I don't know yet. We have to wait and see what happens," Papa said in a defensive voice, stiffening up for some criticism.

"Max, we have to make quick decisions. We have to leave before Hitler comes here," Mother argued. "We're trapped." She glared at Papa. "If we owned a car, we wouldn't be in this mess now."

"How am I supposed to know Hitler was coming today?" he shouted.

The buses were not running and the trains were busy ferrying Belgian soldiers to the battlefields. Papa leafed through the phone book to find the answer, a number to call for a taxi. The lines were busy.

"Hitler can be here in hours, not days," Mama went on, and I could see Sam stiffening.

"Mama, please don't do this to us," Sam pleaded. "This is no time to fight."

"Once he steps into Antwerp, Hitler will be coming after the Jews," Mama said.

My parents had lived in Germany in the early 1920s when Hitler and his Nazi thugs began to unfold their reign of terror, blaming Jews for the country's economic problems. Hitler had roused the Germans, encouraging them to storm into Jewish neighborhoods where they smashed windows and dragged people out of their businesses and homes to beat them up in the streets. My mother remembered the terror of those times. My parents had fled with an infant Sam to Belgium in 1924. "Have you forgotten?" she said to him now.

News came from the radio that hundreds of thousands of British and French troops were rushing to Belgium's rescue. King Leopold addressed the nation. "The fight will be hard. Great sacrifices will be asked of you. But there can be no doubt about the final victory."

In his order of the day, Hitler declared, "Soldiers of the Western Front! The battle, which is beginning today, will decide the fate of the German nation for the next thousand years. Go forward now and do your duty!"

When I began my research into my family's flight from Hitler, I found myself pondering what Hitler and Leopold said that day over the radio and the fact that I was there, literally in the middle of these two historic statements. Yet, the younger me, a child, relished parts of the adventure that was to come.

Papa, a diamond dealer, decided to leave the house when the bombings stopped to collect money that he was due. He had flirted with danger many times. His first memorable brush came during World War I when, as a teenage soldier, he deserted the German army hours before his unit boarded a train to take part in the Battle of Verdun, in France. He made the right choice. More than 700,000 French and German soldiers were killed, wounded, or joined the missing during a battle that came to represent more than any other the horrors of modern warfare.

A train saved him again on 1 September 1939, the day Hitler invaded Poland, interrupting my father's business trip and starting World War II. My father's close escape that day seemed to foreshadow our flight from Belgium.

So, when I was older and the stories were retold to me, I wasn't surprised to learn that Father walked the streets of Antwerp mere hours after the Nazi planes bombed the city. He followed his usual gutsy instincts, eager to catch his clients before they planned to evacuate after the horrifying morning.

He got them all before they scurried away, and as he gingerly picked his way home, ducking the strafing planes, the debris, the fleeing residents, his steps were somehow lighter, his feet almost relieved knowing that he was no longer hobbled by the thought of returning home without cash, and he no longer had to face

Mama's wrath, which, in its immediacy, was certainly more frightening to him than the invasion.

Like most of Antwerp, Papa wanted to leave that first day and came up with an idea that I thought was strange but in hindsight made good sense. He went with my brothers to the Antwerp Zoo, less than a ten-minute walk from our house. As Leo would explain to me years later, "Father figured he might find somebody there with a truck, a worker, a zookeeper, somebody, and hire him to drive us away. But nobody was there. Then we realized, what if the Germans started bombing again and dropped one on the zoo? The tigers and lions might get loose. That would be more dangerous."

As a young child, I didn't know anything that was going on, but I sensed something was awfully wrong. The world that Mama had patterned for me was unraveling. We usually went for a morning walk on Antwerp's main boulevard, the Keyserlei, where fancy stores and well-dressed people dotted the landscape, and street photographers took pictures of us strolling hand-in-hand. On Fridays we'd stop at the neighborhood bakery to buy challahs, the long braided loaves we used to break bread for our meal on the Sabbath. Today there would be no stroll, no family photos, no Sabbath bread.

I later asked my eighty-five-year-old mother, "What kind of day was it when the Nazis came"?

"Friday," she answered.

"No, I didn't mean that," I shot back in annoyance. "Did it rain? Was the sun out? Wasn't it cloudy that day?"

"No, it was nice weather. It was such nice weather," Mama said. "Such a nice day to take a walk."

I had always thought it had been cloudy and windy. I was surprised, and somewhat disappointed, when my mother told me what a clear day it was. I wanted my memory to associate that day with what I thought I saw, and probably with what I felt war should look like—gray, dreary, cold, damp. The remembrances of a child not yet four years old can do funny things, and so it felt natural to associate bad weather with terrible events.

Instead, the day was magnificent; the sun was beginning to show its glow, a blue sky so clear no painting could duplicate its beauty. Even as the sky was scarred momentarily in places by the trails of airplane exhaust, by the falling bombs and the rising smoke, the sky resisted changing its color to mirror the sad scene below.

Concerning that first attack, I would interview Sam and Leo over a two-day period beginning in July 1991: "Were there any signs prior to May 10 that we would be invaded? Did we prepare ourselves, like giving the furniture to someone to keep?

Sam: No, nothing.

Nothing?

Sam: Nothing. It was a complete surprise.

Why was it such a complete surprise? You knew there was a war going on.

Sam: I was a kid. It was a complete surprise. We didn't know that Belgium was going to be invaded.

Leo: The government knew. The people were not informed of anything.

Sam: They suspected, but weren't sure.

What happened on May 10?

Sam: All we saw were airplanes up in the air at six o'clock in the morning bombarding Antwerp.

Did we get hit at all?

Sam: No. Maybe on the outskirts, a few bombs fell.

Leo: Belgium was attacked, and we left on May 12.

Didn't our parents talk about what to do?

Sam: I guess they were discussing what to do. We were all by ourselves. Some people already went Friday. Some people with their own cars left Friday. Right away. They went to the seashore, I think to Ostende. There was a boat to England.

The interview took place in my spacious two-story country-style home sitting comfortably on a sloping hill in suburban Connecticut, framed in the back by woods no more than a pitcher's throw from our deck, and in front, in the distance, by the Sleeping Giant, the name of a nearby mountain that lay stretched on its back for miles and miles. It was a peaceful summer day, one that seemed to call us to come outside, and I felt that's what my brothers wanted to do, rather than be pestered by my questions. I felt I was in a tug-of-war with them. I was peppering them with questions at one end of the rope, while they were struggling hard to keep me at bay with clipped, sharp answers, mistakenly thinking that the few words that rolled through my tape recorder would be enough to appease their lifelong little brother, who, at fifty-four then, was still made to feel so young, a little boy, and so distant from the elder Sam, then sixty-seven, and Leo, sixty-two. It was a constant struggle to stand up to them as an equal. Not even a beautiful home, a successful career, a lovely wife, four handsome sons, or the drink in my hand, could bridge that divide. I felt like I was intruding into their past, not *our* past.

Leo: Thousands of people started leaving, especially those who had cars, and we wondered how we were going to leave and where we were going.

Why did we wait two days before we left?

Leo: Why, who knows why? Because we thought that the Germans would not come in.

Sam: We had no choice. How do you go? You need a car.

Leo: The trains weren't working because they took the soldiers to the front.

Sam: When the Germans came, we decided to leave.

What did we do during the two days?

Leo: Nothing. We sat home and listened to the radio.

What kind of arrangements did we make to leave?

Leo: I don't remember how we decided to leave.

Sam: We took a cab.

Did we observe the Sabbath?

Sam: How could we?

Leo: This I don't remember. We probably did.

Mother told me she had already prepared the meal, cooked it the night before.

Leo: We had to eat anyway.

Did we have a telephone?

Leo: Yes, I still remember the number.

Sam: I don't believe it.

Leo: 925-68.

When did we order the taxi?

Sam: We ordered it on Sunday and Monday we got it.

It's incredible! We stayed in Antwerp for three days?

Sam: Yes, we didn't know what to do. When we heard the Germans were starting to invade we didn't even know there was an invasion going on.

Well, you heard the bombs.

Sam: The bombs, but there was no troop invasion involved.

You listened to the radio.

Sam: Yes, it took awhile. You didn't get information immediately. The government didn't exactly say what's happening.

As I listened to Sam and Leo, I drifted back to May 1940 and considered how the first day's attack changed their lives forever: never to go back to school in Antwerp, to play ball there, or take a stroll in the city's park, gone were any thoughts of holding a girlfriend's hand, or going to the movies with their Belgian friends. They would never again see most of them. Many did not survive.

And I thought about myself, too. I never went to school in Belgium, never had a chance to make friends, to go to the movies there, or to grow up in the country in which I was born. I tried hard to remember those first few days of destruction and confusion, to feel the fright my brothers felt. Was I scared when the bombs poured down like rain on Antwerp and a few days later along the route of our fearsome journey? Will I ever know?

There was little talk in the house that Friday and hardly any anticipation for celebrating the start of the Jewish Sabbath at sundown. Mama had started cooking the night before, and the vapors from the fleshy smell of chicken and the sweet odor of babka were already whetting my appetite. I couldn't wait to dig into a piece of challah, dunk it in a delicious bowl of chicken noodle soup, and relish the mouth-watering taste. Instead, the daily common bread was used to greet the Sabbath. On other Friday nights, the dining room was brightly lit and the good chinaware was set for the festive meal. This time Mama was too drained to be cheery and set the table with the old weekday plates, the patterns on them faded from years of use. Only one light, a dim bulb dangling in the kitchen, was turned on. An enforced blackout buried Belgium in total darkness to protect us from Nazi air raids. Shutters were closed and the drapes were drawn. Yet one tradition Mama would not break—lighting the Sabbath candles.

Mama covered her eyes with the palm of her hands in prayer and recited in Hebrew, "Blessed are You our God, King of the Universe, Who sanctified us with His commandments, and has commanded us to kindle the lights of the Sabbath." The flames danced like butterflies, embracing us with their peaceful glow, and I remember that moment as strange, yet comforting. Papa recited the blessings for the bread and wine in a hushed tone, his voice only distantly related to the voice from the father who had previously sung the Sabbath prayers with booming enthusiasm. He rushed through the rest of the prayer as if he didn't believe its meaning any more. The Sabbath prayer ended with these fitting words, "...cause our light to illuminate that it be not extinguished forever, and let Your favor shine so that we are saved."

On Saturday mornings, Papa's routine was to go to the synagogue with Sam and Leo, while Mama remained at home with me and kept the food warm for lunch. Saturday, 11 May 1940, was different. My parents and brothers started packing as news from the war front filtered through the radio: Belgian troops and the British and French forces were falling back.

Together my parents emptied the cupboards, wrapped newspaper around the dishes and glassware, and packed clothes in suitcases. Our home appeared cold, bleak, a home on the verge of abandonment.

I didn't understand why we had to leave our home while the neighbors remained, not yet knowing the difference between a Jew and a Christian.

"I don't want to go," I pleaded with Mama.

"Mein teier yingl," she said in Yiddish, "we're only going away for a few days."

When I think back now, situated as we were almost within sight of the Germans storming into Belgium, it is inconceivable that Papa allowed Saturday to slip by without picking up the phone. It is inconceivable that he was waiting, waiting until Sunday to make the call, to call for the taxi that would save us. The Torah commands Jews to rest on the seventh day, the Jewish Sabbath, and to refrain from weekday activities. But our lives were in danger. Surely my father, a choir boy for almost ten years at his synagogue, must have known that Jews can break the Sabbath laws if observing them endangers a human life. The Midrash, rabbinical commentaries on the Torah, teaches us: "We should disregard one Sabbath for the sake of saving the life of a person, so that he may observe many Sabbaths." Yet my father didn't call that day.

Chapter 2

THE WAY WE REMEMBER OURSELVES

Before that terrible day of 10 May came, we lived in an apartment, our apartment, on the second floor of a bleak, sandy-colored, slab building wedged between two larger houses overlooking a narrow tree-lined street. Across the street was a railroad track, hidden from view by a high concrete wall that muffled the rumbling sounds of the trains. I slept in the dining room, while Mama and Papa slept at the front of the house in the master bedroom that opened up to a balcony from where I once peed on an old lady's head below. My brothers shared a small bedroom off to the side of the kitchen.

Because I was so much younger than my brothers, I don't recall much of our family before that fateful year. Memory is not always honest, and sometimes it is as if I was born that year, 1940, because the trauma that we went through has cemented the last year in Antwerp most clearly of all of them in my mind.

I remember that I spent most of my time in the front room, playing with my toy train set: an engine, and two passenger cars. I loved hearing the train's rhythmic, gentle chugging sounds, feeling serene and sheltered sitting inside its oval-shaped track. Years later, Leo would tell me more about our surroundings: "We lived in a fairly quiet neighborhood. We had no bathtub, central heating, or refrigerator. A coal stove was used to heat the apartment in the winter. Taking a bath was a discomforting problem. We needed to warm the water on the stove and then pour it into a huge basin, like you see in the old Western movies. Since we were five at home you can imagine how long it took. Father was in the diamond business, and often out of town. Life was a little monotonous in those days. Every Saturday morning we went to synagogue. Saturday afternoons we went walking in the local park where we met friends. On Sunday afternoons I went to the movies with…Sam. I remember seeing the *Dead End Kids*."

At that time Papa was known in his trade as one of the best diamond cutters in Antwerp. His job was to cut and polish rough, brown-looking stones into shiny, sparkling diamonds. His trained eye could tell how to cut a rough diamond, what its color and clarity would be, and how many carats the finished stone would weigh. Sometimes the rough stones had to be cut into smaller parts by other craftsmen, called diamond cleavers, before my father could start his work. These skilled workers split these rough diamonds along pre-marked lines with a diamond-studded tool to remove spots and flaws to get top value.

Papa then took over from the cleavers, and polished the stones using a turntable that revolved at 3600 rpm. The polishing surface was saturated with diamond dust, since the only material known to cut a diamond was another diamond. The combination of the wheel's speed and the fine diamond abrasive allowed him to delicately peel away the stone's rough skin and reveal a brilliant gem underneath.

In order to manipulate the rough against the wheel, he inserted the rough into a set of prongs that resembled fangs. He held the prongs in his right hand and then placed the diamond gently on the wheel's edge. He progressed toward the center, to the slower part of the wheel to give the diamond its smoothest polish. He allowed the diamond to run on the wheel for only a brief moment, constantly checking each cut or facet.

Papa did well for a while, but the Depression sapped even the diamond business. Finally, unable to find enough work in Antwerp, he became fascinated by an offer nearly 1000 miles away in Prague. A jewelry store eager to attract customers hired him to become the store's window display for a gawking public, promoting my father as the best diamond cutter in the world. That move seemed to bring out his dark side. Perhaps it was the flattery of his title? The watching crowds? The feeling that he was once again a man without wife and family? What we knew was only that he was away from home for months at a time. He sent home very little money, not even enough for Mama to pay the rent and buy food. She was forced to borrow money from friends and acquaintances, sending Sam, her teenage son, to fetch it. For Sam, it was a humiliation he always remembered.

Hitler's invasion of Czechoslovakia in March 1939 forced my father to flee Prague. He barely escaped into Poland, where he jumped on a freight train rolling to the Baltic Sea, and hopped on a freighter that almost sank in rough water on its way to Antwerp.

When he returned home, the battles between Mama and Papa were heated. They both yelled a lot, but he always overwhelmed her with his fiery temper, as short and as cutting as the sound of his name, Max. I lost myself in the corner of the front room, playing with my trains to block out their shrill-sounding words as they seemed almost alien to each other, two sides of a war, and locked in a never-ending battle.

Mama soothed her anger and hurt by going on shopping binges. She purchased expensive clothes—for herself and her sons—and the finest tablecloths and linens, all embroidered with Belgian lace. She took care of these possessions as if they were her second children, ironing with the eye of an artist, leaving no trace of wrinkles, and folding and flattening them into perfect rectangulars. The closet was always a quiet scene of order and symmetry, the bed sheets, pillows, and towels arranged in neat stacks. There was also an appearance of order in the lives of her two older boys that centered mostly on school and friends. Sam and Leo attended the Tahkemoni, a Hebrew day school that went up to the seventh grade. My parents believed it was important to ground the boys in the rituals and traditions of Judaism, learning the teachings of the Torah, as well as the regular subjects of mathematics, science, grammar, and history. The Tahkemoni was one of two comprehensive religious schools in Antwerp. At the time of the invasion in May 1940, Leo was in the fifth grade, and Sam, who had already graduated from the Tahkemoni, was attending public high school.

Sam was a typical teenager, though I do remember he stood out among his peers because of his good looks. He had a sensitive face, and a slender body that made him seem taller than he actually was. He looked dapper with his black hair combed backward tightly and a silk shawl draped around his neck and tucked underneath a sweater or shirt.

Though much of this story that I tell draws on Sam's memories, it was hard to pry loose his feelings, particularly because of those painful years when he tried to buffer his two younger brothers from their parents' bitter clashes while, at the same time, trying to be a young man enjoying his teenage years.

Sam's pain was evident even during our interviews: "Fred, please don't write anything about me. It's really not important. Just write about the escapes."

"I understand. If you don't want to talk, that's okay," I said and waited in silence for the next rebuff.

"I did what everybody else did," Sam said. "I went out with friends, we had parties, went to the movies, sometimes just hung around doing nothing in particular, played soccer. What else do you want to know?"

"Did you go out with girls?" I asked.

"Sure, I went out with girls," Sam answered.

What a foolish question, I thought almost as soon as I'd asked it. He looked like a suave young movie star in those days, like a dark, brooding James Dean before there even was a James Dean. Of course there were girls.

Leo was just as handsome, but in an athletic way. He had jet-black, curly hair, was broad-shouldered and stocky, and had a tough, brooding look for his age that could be wiped away with a soft, tight-lipped smile.

I was much closer to him than to Sam, who was two months away from his thirteenth birthday and studying for his bar mitzvah when I was born on 8 October 1936. I didn't even know he existed at times, so far were we from each other's experience of the world; that's how much age drew us apart. It took decades, in fact years more even after the 1991 interview, for Sam and I to close that gap and to see each other as real brothers.

But Leo and I? It was easier during our early years. In Antwerp, he often took me to the park with his friends. Of course, sometimes he'd leave me with the girls while he went off to play a game of pick-up soccer with the guys. Later, he would teach me to ride a two-wheeler, a feat that elevated him to hero status in my eyes.

As an adult, Leo remembered our Passovers in Antwerp most fondly: "Passover was sort of a feast. The day before we changed the Chinaware.... [The Talmud, the code of Jewish law, forbids matzoh and other unleavened products to be tainted by everyday kitchen ware.] Passover was also the time we got new clothes and shoes. In those days we wore Knickerbockers. Papa read the Haggadah at the Seder table."

In reading the Haggadah, Papa told the story of the Jewish people living as slaves in Egypt, Moses guiding them toward freedom, and Egyptian soldiers pursuing them toward the Red Sea, which parted miraculously for the Jews to flee through, and closed up again to drown the former captors. Long before Cecile B. DeMille brought it to life in Technicolor in the movie *The Ten Commandments,* my father brought it to life over our Passover meal, and it was every bit as real as Mr. DeMille's version, with the angel of God traveling like fog through the town, passing over the houses of the faithful who had made the offering of lamb's blood on their doorframes, and taking the firstborn children of those who had not.

My father was a master storyteller, and each Passover the tension was apparent in my family's faces as he again spoke of the Jews fleeing through the gap in the water. Would they make it in time? Would the Egyptians catch them? All my parent's arguments, all their troubles, could be set aside for these rituals and, though they were brief moments in any year, they seasoned our lives with happiness, with the joy of family and the comfort of traditions.

Summer vacations at the beach were also joyful. In August, the traditional month in Europe for vacation, we traveled to the shore along the North Sea. We were among the many Belgian Jews who sunned at coastal towns like Knokke. We stayed at the same place every year, an apartment that was above a fish market, overlooking the sea. My family started going there long before I was born. My two older brothers kept busy enjoying their friends, my parents relaxed in the shade of a cabana near the water.

The casino was Knokke's center attraction, spawning a fashionable nightlife that suited my father's tendency for gambling. August 1939 was our final trip to Knokke. A month later Hitler started World War II, conquering Poland, the country where 3 million Jews lived, more than in any other country in the world.

That was life before the invasion of my homeland. We had our Passover together. We had our apartment in Antwerp with my mother's lovely fine linens. We had our summer vacation. Yet our life as it was, though sometimes turbulent with my parents' arguments, and at times a life idyllic, would not be allowed to stay that way. Hitler's invasion of Czechoslovakia, which brought my father home, even Poland with its 3 million Jews, were not enough to satisfy the snapping jaws and hunger of one man's hatred.

I remember gazing out the window of our summer home that August and saw a British fighter plane dash across the sea, heading eastward, a harbinger of dread.

Chapter 3

ESCAPING FROM ANTWERP

Monday, 13 May 1940, a slim three days after the German invasion of Belgium, the long-awaited taxi arrived to pick us up, and we began the first leg of our six-year journey dodging the Nazis. Hitler was one step away from us on Monday, when we evacuated the apartment and rushed down the stairs to the waiting taxi.

Years later, I pushed my family for details.

What did we do with the belongings?

Mother: I leave everything. I took the luggage to the lady next door. Tablecloths, laundry, I had such beautiful laundry. Clothes and fur coat, everything.

Leo: Everything stayed home. We just left with a suitcase, that's all. You know the house; there was no concierge in the apartment. We rented it from the people who lived downstairs. We left the stuff with them. And then we took a taxi and went to La Panne.

Sam: We took five suitcases and put them on top of the taxi.

What about the photographs?

Mother: We left them behind in the apartment. The landlord kept them.

What did we do with the furniture?

Sam: It stayed there. We didn't realize it was going to go like this, that we're not coming back. Everything remained.

We thought that we would be coming back?

Sam: I suppose so.

What did we take with us?

Mother: Some clothing, pillowcases, schtepdecken, wie sagt man das? How do you say that?

Blankets.

Memories of the minutest details become understandably blurred after decades in slumber. Did we just take one suitcase, or was it more as Sam suggested? Did we tell a landlord to hold our belongings, or the people who lived downstairs, or the lady next door? Were they one and the same? Did we leave Antwerp two days later or was it three days?

Sam: It was two or three days later.

So, we stayed here for two or three days?

Sam: A day or two. I don't remember exactly.

Would Father have known the answers? If only Father had been alive to fill in the missing pieces of my childhood, our adventures, our terrors. I ache every day at the thought of never having asked. I have to beg what I can from my brothers and my mother as well. And yes, even my own small boy's memory provides me with some memories.

Mama and I rushed out of the house and climbed into the backseat of the taxi. Leo and Sam squeezed into fold-down jump seats, that looked like mini leather bar stools, attached to the back of the front seats. Papa slid in on the passenger side next to the cabby. The streets were deserted, shops were boarded up, and it felt like we were the only people left in the city. There was hardly any traffic on the highway. I can remember that.

Did we stop on the way to have lunch?

Leo: Are you kidding? The Germans were coming.

Sam: It took us two hours, from Antwerp to La Panne.

Leo: There were no highways at the time, small roads.

Sam: They had highways in '30, '40, of course, they had highways to the seashore.

Leo: It was quite a smooth ride, I think.

Sam: Absolutely.

Absolutely. Sam said it with such assurance, and it was such a grand understatement, that he made me feel as if we were heading to the beach for a vacation, not running away from a war.

I remember some. About halfway between Antwerp and the English Channel, a memory of a black Nazi fighter plane circling above us doused that feeling of leaving for vacation, if I even had it back then. Didn't I know already in my young mind that something was deeply wrong? The cabby suddenly speeded up, unexpectedly lurching the car forward and causing one of the suitcases to fly off the roof. I turned to look out the back window and watched it tumble on the road, bed sheets and blankets strewn all over. In my mind it flashed. I saw it again. Sam was correct. We took more than one suitcase. The driver didn't bother to stop as we raced toward the seashore. The pilot toyed with our fears for a minute or two before disappearing into the distance, the aircraft looking, to my young eyes peering through the window, like a small, harmless bug.

We were traveling to La Panne, a coastal town about sixty miles from Antwerp, passing through quaint villages famous before the war for summer getaways and its high sand dunes. La Panne was 3 miles from the French border. When we arrived in La Panne, the cab driver stopped and protested to my father that this was as far as he would go, and ordered us out.

"I have to return to my family," he told Papa, who got out his wallet fast as the cabby wanted to leave. "No, no, I don't want it. I have to go now. You can give me as much money as you want. I still won't take you." Our driver was a surly, chunky figure with a crushed, mean-looking face that seemed to make its living being angry. Papa didn't give up, offering more money, thinking the man was simply bluffing for all he could get, something that my father would probably do as well if he were in the driver's seat. The cabby held firm, arguing that he wouldn't be able to plow through the thick crowds of people fleeing from the Nazi onslaught.

"We started walking on the road," Leo would recall later, "the road that was full of people, as far as the eye could see, hundreds of thousands of people. We could hardly advance."

With my family carrying the suitcases that had survived the cab ride, we marched toward France, shoved forward by the huge throng of refugees surrounding us. I remember that I felt caged in by the mounds of overcoats and jackets many wore rather than taking the time to stuff them into trunks or bags, these faceless over-padded wanderers ahead of me, around me, shuffling through the dirt roads and kicking up dust in the face of this little boy who came up just above their knees. And all the while the German fighter planes buzzed above. It was just a crazy, confusing scene: cars honking in panic to cut through the tightly-packed crowd, the vehicles bulging with passengers and belongings, suitcases and bicycles tied to car roofs, trucks jammed with mattresses, clothes and furniture, all of us frantic and getting in the way of Allied troops regrouping for the onrushing Nazis. I had been up since about six o'clock in the morning; I was just a small boy, and I was dead tired, and tired of walking on those pebbled roads. My feet were hurting from the rocks that crawled into my boots. But Mama was holding me tightly with one hand, the other strained by the weight of a suitcase she was carrying; she wouldn't let go of me; she wouldn't let us stop walking.

Later that day Papa sighted an old acquaintance from Antwerp. When he spotted his friend and strode towards him, it seemed the sardine-packed refugees parted to make way for my father; even in this terrible confusion he was that impressive.

Mother: Ya, ya, on the French border, we meet friends there.

What were their names?

Mother: Sammy knows. I don't. And he was with his wife and his mother-in-law and children. And then all of a sudden we rent a truck?

A truck?

Mother (in deep thought): This man, what was his name?

You mean we bought a truck?

Mother: That I don't know…and he could drive.

Sam: In La Panne, there were two families in the car. We were there with nine, ten people in the car.

Who was the family? Do you remember?

Sam: Sure. Stolz.

They had five in the car?

Sam: Ach, they had more. The three boys…they had at least five people.

Papa pushed through the crowd to get closer to the man.

"Stolz, Stolz," Papa yelled to get his attention before he got lost in the chaos. Stolz spun around.

"Gross, Gross, can you believe this? This is insane. It's unbelievable. Look at all these people." He was in a panic. "My mother-in-law can hardly move. She's old and weak."

Papa's mind was on getting himself and his family through this alive without surrendering to the shock of the moment, careful not to be slowed down by emotional chatter.

"Let's get a car," Papa directed Stolz. "I can't drive, but I have some money."

When my mother, brothers, and I caught up with Papa and the Stolzes, the two families sat down by the side of the road, deciding whether to dump their belongings before marching on.

"I know how to drive and I have some money, too. We'll buy it together." Stolz's spirit was rising, but in an instant it fell to the floor. "But where? Everybody living around here is on the road. There's probably nothing open."

"We'll find somebody, a farmer or a mechanic. They'll sell anything now because they need the cash." Father was determined. "The car has to be big enough for two families."

"I don't care how big it is," Stolz responded.

Mother: We all went into a truck. It was like a big taxi and he drove, and on the French border the planes were flying. Every time they came, we had to go out of the car and lay down on the ground, and then they left.

Leo: It was a beautiful car.

Sam: It was a huge Nash.

It was black, wasn't it?

Leo: No, it wasn't. It was beige brown.

Sam: Yes, beige brown, a seven-seater.

Arrangements were made between the two families to buy the car?

Leo: We bought the car together.

Sam: Stolz was the only one who knew how to drive. Stolz was the driver.

So, they each paid for the car?

Sam: Yes, it was a few thousand francs. At the most $200. It was an old car, 1930-something.

Leo: You could get a lot of money today for it.

Sam: Oh, yeah. I bet now. Oy, oy, oy!

Who did we buy the car from?

Sam: A garage.

So, from La Panne we took the car?

Sam: We stayed in La Panne. We slept there.

Leo: We slept in a garage, or on a farm.

How many days?

Leo: Two days, three days, I don't remember.

Sam: Not on a farm, in hay.

In a barn. The farmer let us sleep there?

Leo: Why not? The roads were packed with refugees, miles and miles of refugees, walking, riding in cars.

No kidding?

Leo: Sure, just like you see in the movies sometimes.

Were there soldiers?

Leo: French soldiers.

Sam: They were retreating.

Leo: The roads were packed with refugees, miles and miles of refugees. We figured if we wait a few days, maybe it won't be so crowded and we can drive through.

Sam: Two days for sure we stayed in La Panne. Then we heard the Germans kept on advancing. That's when we left with the car.

On 16 May 1940, retreating French soldiers warned us not to stay around a single day longer. Looking ragged and tired, these soldiers had had enough of war and had joined the ranks of the marching refugees. They somberly reported that Holland had already surrendered and that Nazi units were storming across the Dutch-Belgian border, while more troops cut through the belly of Belgium on a straight line to the coast, with more German tanks and troops sweeping across northern France and looping up toward the Belgian side of the North Sea. They were closing in from three sides and setting a trap for all of us—the millions of fleeing civilians and retreating soldiers—all of us with our backs against the sea. The Gross and Stolz families packed into the old Nash and crossed the border into France, hardly moving faster than the refugees on foot.

Leo: One night when we were bombed, we had to jump in the ditches because they started to machinegun the people on the road, the Germans, they shot from the planes. This was in France, along the French border.

Did we go through Dunkirk?

Leo: Oh, yes.

Sam: We passed Dunkirk, we just passed it.

Leo: No, we heard bombardments there.

Sam: We heard bombardments?

Leo: Big bombardments in Dunkirk. That's where the English retreated.

Did you see the soldiers retreat?

Leo: Yes.

Then what happened?

Leo: Sneak attacks by the Nazi fighter planes.

Sam: No, we continued.

Leo: We passed through Dunkirk where the British retreated and we saw thousands of soldiers heading to the beaches.

Describe the scene to me. What was it like?

Leo: It was, what should I say, it was apocalyptic because you had the bombs falling further up, and the planes over you, and the people didn't know where to go.

Was there a lot of panic?

Leo: Sure, people panicked. They didn't know where to hide.

What did we do at night?

Leo: This is exactly fifty years ago. This I don't remember. We slept in small hotels. Some slept in cars, some in wagons. Some of them had horse buggies. If I knew you wanted to write a book, I would have taken notes.

He scorched me with that remark, blindsided me with it. I felt my face turning a maddening red, my body tightening up, but I understood that looking back fifty years made it impossible to reconstruct one's memory perfectly.

Instead, I took a deep breath and listened carefully to Leo, trying hard to form a picture of the battle scenes. I imagined huge plumes of black smoke staining the blue sky, heard what sounded like a long series of thunderclaps as the bombs exploded upon impact, the ground trembling. I tried to imagine the Nazi planes, with the machine guns sticking out from their wings, diving down on us. But all I really heard were the sounds of my family's voices retelling their alarming adventures, adventures that often were only shadow memories to the small boy I had been at the time. I was envious of Sam, and Leo, and Mama, because they remembered.

The Stukas were the most feared aircraft. Their landing gear was equipped with whistles encased in what looked like small tin cans. We came to know the Stukas that day at Dunkirk. The high-pitched, ear-piercing sounds sent a wave of terror through us as waves of these fighter planes dove to tree-top level at speeds of over 300 miles an hour with their machine guns firing at us. Even when the planes swung back up the tail gunners continued to shoot, sweeping the roads and air with bullets.

We all scrambled into the fields and ditches. Mama dragged me out of the car, across the road, running every which way for a hiding place that was not there. Bodies were sprawled on the roads and in the fields, pools of blood around them. Homes were burning, collapsing. Not even the cows were spared, as they lay dead in the field. Mama held my hand tightly in hers, afraid that the crowd would sweep me up and I would be lost forever.

Mama: We were driving through Calais, and the planes were flying over us. When the bombs were being dropped, we lay down on the ground. I threw you into a ditch and covered you with my body.

That I remembered. In fact, that was the only crystal clear memory I had of the first few days of the war. I could still see the view I had from mid-air as my mother lifted me: suddenly there was me looking down at the ditch below before darkness closed in when Mother fell heavily on top of me, pushing us into the dirt.

Chapter 4

NACHA'S EARLIER JOURNEYS

My mother was never an affectionate woman. Whenever I hugged her, her body stiffened, like she was protecting herself. Her kisses were cordial, as if she was politely greeting a guest at a party. When she grieved about leaving behind her beautiful laundry the day we fled our home in Antwerp, I had an overwhelming need to embrace her. Yet somehow I knew this would be as unwelcome as the loss of the precious laundry. The best that I could marshal was a gentle touch on her hand.

I remember that we held hands then for a few long minutes, not saying a word to each other. She was in deep thought as her eyes roamed around the tiny apartment she had lived in during the last two years of her life. She bit down on her lips as if to keep her thoughts from slipping out. This reserved, almost cold woman, would be the same woman who wouldn't even hesitate to cover my body with hers that day when the Stukas strafed us with their machine guns.

I hardly knew my mother. Nacha came from Poland. She had mentioned that she lived in Lodz, so I assumed that's where she was born. But a copy of her birth certificate showed that she was born outside of Lodz, in Pabianice, a rural community where some 8,000 Jews lived before the Holocaust.

The daughter of Rachel and Samuel Reichert, my mother came from a country that was sliced into three pieces, one taken over by Russia, the other by Prussia, and the third by Austria. She grew up in the Russian territory, which was ruled by a czar who made life horrible for the Polish people. His vicious militia of volunteer soldiers riding on horseback, called Cossacks, killed hundreds of Polish peasants who had been protesting against their poor living conditions. Too weak to revolt against the Russians, the peasants took their anger out at the Jews, blaming them for their troubles. Hundreds of Jews were killed in a series of massacres called pogroms, a Russian word for the organized persecution of an ethnic group. The wholesale killings of the pogroms were nowhere near as awful as the efficient killing machine of Nazi Germany. Still the killings were barbaric. The Polish people simply beat up Jews, looted their homes, burned down their villages, and butchered them to death with hacksaws, knives, and swords.

When asked about it my mother said, "They rode on horses, and with sword in hand slaughtered the Jews on the streets," and the look in her eyes told me that she was still witnessing the murders with the eyes as a child.

Mama talked about her childhood in short sentences, but the tone in her voice was one of longing for something that never was to be, and that, I believe, was simply to have had a normal childhood. And, yet, as I paused to reflect on her life between her silent moments, I wondered whether my own thoughts, my own longings, were being projected onto my mother. Was it my longing for a normal childhood? She was four years old when they rode horses and came to kill; I was three years old when they flew planes that also came to kill.

I tried hard to penetrate her private world, but she would only let me in only a little. She explained that her father died when he was in his forties. She was nine years old and she had a baby brother named Aaron. I had never known this before the

1988 interview. Both her father and brother died of tuberculosis around 1912, she told me. Her brother was four years old.

Soon after, she and her mother Rachel moved to Leipzig, Germany. Two years later, World War I broke out. Germany declared war on France, Belgium, and England. Rachel and her daughter, Nacha, lived in a rundown apartment in the Jewish section of town. They both worked in a millinery shop making ladies' hats. The job paid pennies a day, and both had to work long hours to survive. My mother had no time to go to school. Germany suffered heavy losses on the battlefields; the economy in the homeland was in a shambles, and people went begging for food. My grandmother was lucky to have had a job, but that's not the way she wanted to live. Rachel was a beautiful woman in her late thirties. Her perfectly chiseled face, high cheekbones, and determined eyes attracted a clothing salesman from Switzerland. A widower, he came to Leipzig in search of a wife and met my grandmother one Sabbath at the synagogue. Their overwhelming needs became a perfect match.

The clothing salesman wanted a showcase woman, and she simply craved for a safe place to live. There was one hitch: her thirteen-year-old daughter, my mother. Rachel's new love wanted nothing to do with this beautiful child, despite her oval, smooth-as-silk face and the predictably sad expression that seemed to foretell her misfortunes in later life. Faced with the choice of abandoning her daughter or giving up what she must have seen as her chance for a better life, Rachel chose Abraham and sacrificed her own flesh and blood to the dark and lonely care of a Jewish orphan home. They married and hopped on a train for Switzerland.

When my brothers and I learned about this after she died, we were dumbstruck.

Sam: I don't understand why she left her alone. I don't see what she saw in him.

I didn't understand either. But, then I didn't understand when my mother, too, had let me go, to live with a foster family later in our journey. I wanted to shout so loud that the nearby trees would have been torn from their roots. Then, in hindsight, as I was writing about that part of my life, I understood why she gave me away. While her mother imprisoned her in an orphanage and left her forever, she released me from an actual prison, a prison that she feared would be the next to last stop to death. But that part of the story is mine, and this part is hers.

Abraham, my step-grandfather, was a peddler in Switzerland. Accompanied by Rachel, he went from village to village, lugging his wares on his back or carting them in a carriage, summoning the townspeople with, "Old clothes for sale, old clothes for sale." Many eastern European Jews who fled the pogroms did that kind of work, or were forced to beg for money. Hitler hated those Jews, and in fact, turned witness against one who was arrested for begging. That incident occurred in 1908 when Hitler was an unknown, rejected artist. He told his roommate, "I have joined the Anti-Semitic League," which was a hate group bent on doing violence against Jews who lived in Vienna, Austria, his native country.

Mama never mentioned what actually happened to her in Leipzig. I knew that Rachel remarried and moved to Switzerland, and I had always accepted my mother's reason for staying behind: "I couldn't get a passport because the Germans wouldn't allow me to leave."

Later, I discovered the truth. My mother had a special bond with Ita, her only granddaughter. This bond arose out of a mutual understanding of the enduring pain of abandonment. It all comes back to me now. I remember Mama taking the one-hour subway ride from Queens to upper Manhattan in the wintry storms to be with her baby grandchild, a baby girl adopted by my brother Sam and his wife a few weeks after Ita was born to a teenage mother. And so years later, I imagine Mama relating to Ita her own teenage story, weaving into it the painful memory of the day she and her mother parted, confiding in Ita that her stepfather, Abraham, simply wanted nothing to do with her.

My mother didn't even tell me she was placed in an orphanage. When I looked through her possessions after she died, I found an autograph book that contained notes from her friends in the orphan home. The discovery exposed a dark, secluded world my mother hid from me. And like much of her life, the autograph book was hidden in a withered leather hatbox underneath some brightly colored shawls she loved to wear over her head in the heat of the day. I cried hard at the thought of her living in an orphanage, and between the tears understood why Mama hurt so much. The pages of notes signed by her orphaned friends are safely in Ita's hands now.

There was no record of when she left the orphanage, though she mentioned she moved to Frankfurt soon after Germany surrendered in November 1918 to end World War I. In Frankfurt, she stayed in an apartment with a girlfriend who was most likely from the orphan's home. It was in this city, the birthplace of its most famous writer, Goethe, that my father began to court her.

At the time my mother was adjusting to life at the orphanage, a German soldier was taking a furlough from the trenches on the Belgian front to sightsee in Leipzig. He toured

St. Thomas's Church, where Martin Luther delivered his first sermon and where Johann Sebastian Bach had played the organ and is buried there. But the soldier was more impressed with a massive 300-foot monument of the Battle of the Nations, honoring the war dead and celebrating Germany's victory over Napoleon's France in Leipzig in 1813. "This has nothing to do with art," the lowly corporal noted, "but it is enormous and beautiful."

The soldier was Adolf Hitler, who dreamed of becoming a giant in art and architecture, but failed twice to be admitted to the Vienna Academy of Fine Arts. If he could have found acceptance in the art world, would he have felt the need to seek out a more deadly medium of expression?

After thinking about the Stukas barreling down on us in Dunkirk, and learning so much of my own history, in retrospect it seems to me that he was beginning to stalk our family as far back as 1917.

road, hoping that we wouldn't get killed. The people were running off the road throwing themselves into the fields and the ditches. We didn't want to leave the car because we were afraid someone would steal it even without gas in it. There was fire all around us, houses were burning, trees were in flames, and the smoke from the bombings made it look like night. After about a half hour, we were still waiting for Father to return. We thought he was either lost or died somewhere on the road looking for gasoline. The bombings didn't go on all the time. The planes just came and went."

As we waited for Papa, the Luftwaffe, the German Air Force, continued to pound us, while the Nazi ground forces and tank divisions powered through Belgium, overcoming fierce resistance from British and French forces, and sweeping toward the millions of people stuck along the coastline like wet sand clinging to feet, among them the Gross and the Stolz families.

"There he is, there he is," shouted Mama in German, running toward Papa, still steady on his feet, soot from the fallout of the bombardments blanketing his clothes, the can of gasoline firmly in his hand. "Thank God, you came back. We thought you were never coming back, that you were dead somewhere on the road."

"I didn't even think about not coming back," Father replied.

Stolz drove slowly through the throng of refugees as the Stukas continued to spatter the roads with machine gun fire and bombed the surrounding villages.

The next day, 17 May, the Nazi Panzer tanks, led by the legendary German Field Marshal Erwin Rommel, advanced furiously through northern France, knocking off the Allied tanks like bowling pins, reaching Cambrai, about 25 miles south of

Chapter 5

THE NAZI LUFTWAFFE ATTACKS US ON THE ROAD

When the air attacks stopped, my mother lifted herself, and then me, from the ditch. In a daze; we made our way quickly back into the car to continue our journey with the Stolzes. It was 16 May.

Leo: We kept on going, but once we ran out of gasoline, and father said 'I'm going to the next town to get some.' We got stuck somewhere between Dunkirk and Abbeville. We almost lost father and thank God we found him and that he came back with some gasoline.

How did he get gasoline?

Leo: I think he got a can some place, picked one up on the road.

So, he came back with gasoline to where we were stuck?

Leo: Yes, he came back to where we were, on the road, on the road; we were stuck on the road.

About an hour later?

Leo: Two hours later. One hour going and one hour coming back. We were all waiting in the car. We were scared. The Germans were bombarding the roads.

And we didn't get hit?

Leo: No, we didn't get hit. We were lucky.

Sam: It was the scariest thing I ever went through. The planes were shooting down at the people, and we were all crammed into the car. And we were stuck in the middle of the

the Belgian border. We were somewhere between Calais and Boulogne, about 125 miles from Rommel's forces. Of course, we didn't know exactly where the Nazis were in relation to our position. Not knowing this added to our fears; our nerves were already threadbare when we ran into more car trouble about an hour after we resumed our ride.

We were outside of Boulogne when the car sputtered, jerked back and forth as if in its dying throes, and suddenly stopped after a few more jolts. Papa jumped out of the car and began to dump our belongings to lighten the load on the engine. "No, Max, don't do that," Mama insisted. "We need the blankets and clothes, and the underwear." The Stolzes looked on in disbelief at Mother's demands as they started throwing their belongings to the side of the road. "I don't understand why you want to hold on to these things," Father retorted. "This is nonsense."

"You never know when we might need them. What are we going to do if Freddy wets his pants?"

"Let's store them someplace," said Papa, finding a solution that helped Mama quiet her fears of never returning home with her belongings.

Stolz frantically pumped the gas pedal to get it started, finally bringing the car back to life with the help of some able-bodied refugees pushing from behind.

Driving further down the northwestern coast, we stopped at Paris-Plage, a small beach resort, and were able to find a warehouse to store our luggage. From that point on, all we had with us were the clothes on our backs.

By late afternoon on 17 May, we made it into Abbeville. The Nash was on its last leg, and all of us were wound tighter than a steel coil from the grueling trip and from dodging the spraying machine guns raining down from the sky. We headed to the first hotel we saw.

Leo: We kept on going until we got to Abbeville.

Then what happened in Abbeville?

Leo: The car got stuck.

Sam: In Abbeville the car got stuck, and was repaired. I remember Stolz asking me if I wanted to drive the car to the garage. I drove the car. The first time in my life I drove a car. It was an adventure. I knew how to drive the car. I brought the car back from the mechanic to the hotel where we were. In Abbeville, we were in a little hotel, like a bed and breakfast.

Leo: Yes, I remember.

Sam: With the Stolzes.

Leo: Very small pension de familie bed and breakfast. Just overnight.

Sam: Not only this. The Stolzes stayed at the hotel the next morning. They said they had to eat. We wanted to continue. We just walked away. The car wasn't running anymore. The distributor cracked. But they wanted to eat. They wanted a whole big meal. Okay, so we left, that's all. We didn't want to wait; we were scared to stay.

Wait a minute. We had to eat, too.

Sam: Nah, it wasn't so important. They wanted a whole big meal.

We ate at the pension?

Leo: Yes, we ate at the pension. I remember even the potage we ate.

What was it?

Leo: Vegetable soup. I have such good memory about it. I remember the street the hotel was on, the street, a dirty street. Ach.

Sam: They had to eat. We wanted to continue. The car wasn't running anymore. We never saw them again.

Did Father get panicky when the car broke down?

Sam. No, why should he be panicky? What for? Nobody was panicky. We did the best we could. There were no bombs falling then. We just had to find a way to get out. Once you found a way to get out, you didn't know what was happening. You didn't know the Germans were almost behind you. You had no idea. You figured maybe the Germans are a thousand miles away.

Why were there no German bombs falling? Why was it so peaceful the night of 17 May? I had to find out.

We wanted to flee to Amiens, about 50 miles southeast of Abbeville, but the French soldiers informed us that German tanks were pummeling their way through the fields toward that town, ready to strike a deadly blow against the French and British forces. And then, poised, as the Germans were, to close all escape routes and trap not only Allied troops but also the millions of refugees, the Nazis suddenly halted their advance at Hitler's order.

Historians later labeled this Hitler's first great mistake of the war. General Franz Halder, chief of the German army, observed in his diary: "Rather unpleasant day. The Führer is terribly nervous. Frightened by his own success, he is afraid to take any chance and would rather pull the reins on us." The entry date was 17 May. Hitler was afraid that his tanks would get stuck in the historically marsh-laden terrains of West Flanders in southwestern Belgium, in the Nazis' haste to reach the sea. In fact, Hitler remembered from his World War I service in Belgium the wear and tear on armament that had been stuck in the patchy ground of streams and moats that engulfed Flanders, the name Flanders itself believed to mean "lowland" or "flooded land." I wonder if Hitler also knew about the Battle of the Great Spurs in 1302 when thousands of untrained Belgian militiamen in defense of their country lured a disciplined French cavalry into these same soggy fields. In any case, Hitler chose to pause. And many, myself included, may be alive today because of his error.

We departed from Abbeville in the dark-blue morning of 18 May, Mama holding my hand as I walked beside her. During our escape, she said many times what a good boy I was, praising me for hardly making a fuss. I remember little about myself then, though I think the sights and sounds of those planes must have mortified me. I was wearing knicker pants, boots, and a tiny topcoat the morning that we marched back to the road, the clothes that I had on when we left Antwerp. As we walked I spotted a Gothic cathedral that sat in the center of a huge field of grass. I know we all walked together, but I remember this so vividly I felt I was alone. It was so quiet as I approached the church, its high towers and sharp edges beginning to take shape against the new day as the darkness of night began to fade. There seemed to be no one around me, just the cathedral and me, and then, as always, it seemed, there was again the touch of my mother's hand in mine. We walked toward the church, hoping that a priest or nun would hide us. I can still see Papa knocking hard on the thick wooden door. No answer.

Leo: We continued to walk on the main road with thousands of refugees. Then a truck passed by and picked us up. It was full of refugees.

What about the other refugees who were walking?

40

Leo: We were worried about ourselves, not the others.

Sam: There was a whole column of people, thousands and thousands and thousands of people walking.

As we rode, we saw piles of clothing, linens, cardboard boxes filled with all kinds of things, fancy and beaten-up luggage abandoned by their owners, who were worrying more about saving their lives than about keeping possessions.

Too soon after our brief respite, the Nazi planes carrying their deadly weapons came into full view.

Sam: In the middle of the road, we were strafed again and ran into a ditch. It was about ten minutes before the planes left. It was a scary moment, I must admit, with all those planes passing by.

Were the planes flying high or low?

Sam: Not too high, not too high, and when it was finished, we climbed back up on the truck, and then we heard there were some casualties from the troops passing by. There were some deaths ahead of us.

Troops passing by us, these were French and British soldiers fleeing to the coast to escape from the onrushing Germans, who were only 45 miles away from where we were at Abbeville. Hearing reports of the advancing Germans from the retreating French and British soldiers, the driver of the pickup truck turned west toward the small coastal town of Le Treport, 35 miles outside of Abbeville. Before the war, Le Treport had been a popular bathing resort for Parisians.

The ride was slow and noisy, the tires digging into the dirt road. Under the falling bombs, the once peaceful seaside towns and villages of Roman-tiled stone houses with well-preserved gardens that artists such as Henri Matisse had captured in paintings, crumbled to the ground.

Chapter 6

Max and His Family

I know much more about my father than I ever did about my mother.

Max Gross was born in Frankfurt, Germany, though he was never a German citizen. He was a citizen of Poland, or so I learned when I came across my parents' French identification cards, which listed an individual's nationality.

I had always assumed his ID card would say German because his name was German. Then I started wondering; maybe when his family moved to Germany, they changed their last name from Grotsky, or Grosviecz, or something like that, to Gross. But that's not the story. The German-sounding Gross was always the family name. I discovered that my father's ancestors were indeed Germans, Germans who fled that country in the fourteenth century because of Jewish persecution.

There was a time when Jews and Christians had lived and worked together without strife for centuries. And when I think of it I imagine men and women dressed in medieval clothes, playing the lute and singing songs, the men wielding shiny lances and riding noble steeds, and the ladies cheering them on. Life was good for the Jews then. They had the right to own land and bear arms, and participated as active members of their communities. Jews were merchants, artists, doctors, lawyers, clerks, and engaged freely in business ventures with Christians. Relationships with their non-Jewish neighbors were mostly very friendly.

Fourteenth-century Germany turned the good life into a nightmare. The country was increasingly dominated by feudal lords, who owned large tracts of land and looked down on the lower class people, feeding them poorly and forcing them into hard labor. Because these peasants were too weak to fight back against the ruling powers, they directed their anger toward the Jews, just as the Germans prior to World War II would do when they went hungry and were unemployed.

Peasants hunted down the Jews, tortured and murdered them, and robbed them of their possessions. Feudal lords watched in silence and took no action to stop it, like many non-Jews did during the Nazis extermination of the Jews. Medieval rulers forced Jews to live in ghettoes, separate quarters of a city marked for Jewish residence, barred them from holding respectable jobs and from owning land. These restrictions forced Jews into marginal occupations that Christians considered socially inferior, particularly lending money on interest, or usury, which the Church banned for its followers. The Church considered charging interest a heresy and "detestable to man and God," its practitioners greedy. Thus, the stereotype of the greedy Jew began, further fueling anti-Semitism. Later, as the Church recognized usury as a necessary financial tool, the Church attempted to expel Jews from the growing banking industry.

But the most serious charge leveled unjustly against the Jews, even before the fourteenth century, was that they were responsible for Jesus' death, a myth that has repeatedly cost Jewish lives. Fortunately, most present-day scholars recognize that the Romans most likely crucified Jesus as a political threat.

Adding to the increasing hatred of Jews in those days was the Black Death, the bubonic plague that swept throughout Germany and the world. The Black Death killed some 25 million Europeans between 1347 and 1351, and tens of millions in other parts of the world. The disease got its name from hemorrhages that turned black and struck the lungs. European Gentiles accused the Jews of transmitting the disease by poisoning the water and the wells. In retaliation, mobs throughout Europe massacred thousands of Jews in the German cities of Frankfurt, Mainz, Cologne, Worms, and elsewhere on the continent, including Switzerland.

Many German Jews escaped to the east, primarily to Poland, the Gross family among them. There, Jews were received with open arms and granted all rights and privileges because the Polish towns needed the new tradesmen and artisans to help boost local economies.

The town where Papa's ancestors settled was named Kolbuszowa, which lies in the part of Poland then occupied by Austria-Hungary. The town was named after a bandit Kolbus who lived in the eleventh or twelfth century. Kolbus and his gang of criminals robbed peasant and nobleman alike. Everybody in that wilderness region was afraid of Kolbus, except for the nobleman who owned the area, Count Tarnowsky. The count organized a posse to track down the bandit, and, after capturing him, hanged him in the woods, the very woods that would become home to such wandering Jews as the Grosses. Centuries later, in July 1942, Hitler's terrorist group, the SS (Schutzstaffel), dragged the town's 1,800 Jews from their homes to the killing camps and gunned down 250 of them in that same forest, continuing the region's bloody traditions.

I was named after my grandfather, Feivel, Yiddish for Fred. Feivel was born in 1860 in Kolbuszowa, the center of Poland's woodworking industry. The Kolbuszowa of my grandfather's time was surrounded by huge, dense stands of oak trees. Feivel and other village artisans earned their living building quality furniture and wagon wheels.

"When he was young, he showed a fine talent in art, and for a while worked as a woodcarver," Hedwig, his youngest child remembered.

In the early 1880s, Feivel married a local woman, Gisele Kurz. They had six sons and three daughters. Joseph, Rosa, Malie, Naftalie, Salomon, and Hermann were born in Kolbuszowa. In 1895, Feivel and his family fled the Polish pogroms to Germany. The fraternal twins Max, and Emil, and Hedwig were born in Frankfurt, Germany. Feivel and Gisele, and their Polish-born children left behind the name-calling and beatings and the persistent accusations that the Jews had killed Jesus. Jews were called "disgusting locusts," "filthy insects," they were a "swamp," a "plague" on Poland.

Yet another forced relocation for the Gross family. And there would be more.

In Germany, Feivel met another kind of resistance, based more on social status than religion. The well-bred German Jews, and also the non-Jews, despised the eastern European Jews who fled to their country. These Jews were the minor artisans, the blue-collar workers and the traveling salesmen of their time, similar to the descendants who fled Germany in the earlier centuries. Still, Feivel and his large family lived better than the Jews who remained in Poland. At least they were left alone and not beaten and murdered in their homes and on the streets.

The Gross family lived comfortably in Frankfurt, renting a spacious and elegant apartment. A huge chandelier hung above an enormous, darkly appointed hallway that lead into a living room decorated with harsh brown wallpaper, a sofa with faded floral upholstery, and chairs with wine-red upholstery and thick padding standing firmly on stumpy bent legs.

The apartment's chandelier entranced dozens of children and grandchildren, especially Joseph's oldest son, Sam, who as a young boy lived with his grandparents for a few years. "I noticed that someone flicked a switch and the chandelier suspended from the ceiling became lit," recalled cousin Sam, decades later. "I had never seen this before, and I set about figuring out this piece of magic. There was obviously a connection between the switch and the light, and I concluded that it must have been done with wires. Sure enough, the next morning, upon close inspection, I found covered wires sneaked along the chain that held the fixture."

That chandelier must have absorbed thousands of stories told in that home. Sometimes, Papa would tell me a story from his childhood, about coaxing his brothers through the partially open doorway only to soak them with a bucket of water that was precariously balanced above on the door edge. He always ended the story with a triumphant childlike laugh. For those of us who lost so much of our families to the Nazis, I think it must be common to be jealous of those inanimate objects that witnessed those precious happy family moments that were forever stolen from us.

Hedwig, his sister, remembered my father years later: "Max was the family cut-up. He never took anything seriously. Emil, his twin brother, was much more serious."

When Feivel moved to Germany, he brought with him his passion for wood carving and became a well-known sculptor in Frankfurt, home of the Rothschilds, the famous international banking family. Raising themselves from the poverty of Frankfurt's Jewish ghetto, the Rothschilds founded the banking firm in the late 1700s, and opened branches in London, Paris, Vienna, and Naples. They became the world's richest family. And they were patrons of the arts—and had heard of my grandfather's talent.

I looked to Aunt Hedwig to tell me about him too: "Your grandfather Feivel was a wonderful man, loved and respected by all who knew him. No one could say anything harsh about him. His talent was recognized, and, because he was well liked, an effort was made to get him a scholarship so he could study art."

The Rothschilds offered him such a scholarship. Feivel accepted it and went to study art at the Stadel Museum. There he learned to make blocks of oak into works of art, and one such beautiful piece was a carved inkwell he sculpted for Baron Rothschild to give as a gift to Kaiser Wilhelm, the emperor of Germany. Other works included sculptures of four cherubs representing the seasons, one shown with a puffy face and sleepy eyes, holding a sickle in her left hand, wearing a floppy hat and pulling up a blanket to cover her from the oncoming cold. It is displayed in my living room. There was also a bas-relief of a flower arrangement and one of an ancient battle of the Crusades. These pieces, plus a few other works, survived two wars, and Feivel and Gisele's children going their separate ways.

While he attended art school, Feivel stood out because of his long, flowing beard and curly sidelocks (called payes in Hebrew), which were the habits of very observant Jews. The sidelocks are supposed to grow to the top of the cheekbone and be worn in front of the ear to be visible. Ashamed to be seen that way, he shaved off his locks and beard, only to be scolded by his art teacher for doing so, according to his young daughter-in-law, my mother.

Well, the art teacher was non-Jewish and so he might not have understood. Feivel, smitten by an artistic award from one of Europe's most powerful families, was desperate for the family's attention and acceptance of him as a potentially famous sculptor. The incident at the art class was just part of Grandfather's struggle with the two faces of Judaism in Germany, the Reform and the Orthodox. The Reform Jews thought of themselves as Germans first and attended fancy synagogues located on beautiful tree-lined avenues. On entering these temples, men and women were handed prayer books and ushers checked their coats for them. The most prominent Jews were given stovepipe hats to wear, and as they and others stepped into the sanctuary, a large choir singing hymns greeted them.

Unfortunately, Feivel did not make much money as an artist, nor did he earn the recognition that could have gained him entrance into a lifestyle that would have separated him from ordinary people. Again I looked to Aunt Hedwig to fill in the details: "He became a butcher, but that was not his training. He was skilled in sculpting. He had an artistic nature. He loved beauty, everything that was pure. But he was not a businessman. He was an artist, but it paid too poorly, so he opened a butcher shop. But no one should say he was a butcher. It did not match his personality." His youngest son, Max, my father, rode his bicycle to deliver the butcher's meat to his customers.

Though Feivel grew back his beard and payes, he could not entirely shed his interest in modern Judaism, and so belonged to two synagogues. One was a shtibel, an improvised house of prayer in someone's home. There the men covered their heads and shoulders in the tallis, wore black hats, and rocked back and forth in prayer and song to give expression to their feelings. A curtain separated the men from the women, an Orthodox custom, so no one would be distracted from prayer. The seats were old, rusty folding chairs, and the windows were covered with heavy, drab drapery.

The other was the more prestigious Börneplatz Synagogue, in Italian Renaissance style and featuring a Moorish dome. On back of a photo of Börneplatz, I found brief notations in my father's handwriting that shed more light into how my grandfather's synagogue choice affected my father's character. Papa was a choirboy from 1903 to 1911, from the age of six to fourteen. Papa also noted two other milestones that occurred at the synagogue: his bar mitzvah in 1910 and his marriage to my mother in 1923.

On 10 November 1938, the Germans burned down Börneplatz. It was among the more than 1,000 synagogues destroyed during Kristallnacht, the Night of Broken Glass, marking the beginning of the Holocaust, the destruction of European Jewry. A plaque now marks the spot where Börneplatz stood.

During my father's childhood, though, Börneplatz was their temple for the Sabbath and Jewish holidays. Feivel's wife, Gisele, would send her husband and children off to shul with the standard Sabbath breakfast of milk and raisin coffee cake churning in their stomachs. The cake was baked in a pan with spirals and a hole in the middle. The pan, a grandchild remembered, was enameled with a not-too-pleasing speckled blue, but the cake was always a delight.

Sabbath afternoons were also special delights for Feivel's grandchildren. They would surround their grandfather as he read them Bible stories, at times stopping to ask them questions and praising them for learning well.

The stark contrast between my mother's and father's early years was as deep and wide as the Grand Canyon, and I wandered whether a huge part of my mother's attraction to her future husband was a secret longing for family.

"Oh, Freddy, he always took care of me so well," my mother always said about Feivel, and the meaning of these words became clearer to me now than when she uttered them.

And Gisele, her mother-in-law? How did she compare to Nacha's Rachel? I would never ask, though I often wondered. According to her youngest daughter, Hedwig, my aunt, Grandma Gisele was an angel. She worked a great deal in charitable causes, visiting the sick and helping the poor. She trained her youngest daughter to do the same. Hedwig once remembered Gisele, a kindergarten teacher, sending her out to the streets to collect money for a poor girl who was getting married and needed a wedding dress: "She was always like that. My mother always had the house filled with people. When refugees came from Poland, everybody slept in my parents' house. My parents were not rich people, but everybody got to eat and a place to sleep. My mother had a golden heart."

Aunt Hedwig inherited her mother's charitable trait. It would save the lives of her husband, Sam, and son, Manfred, during the Holocaust, when the French police rounded up Jews for deportation to the death camps. But that's for later in our story.

Young Max attended a private Jewish school in Frankfurt, where children learned the discipline of respect, and were ruled by teachers who frightened students into behaving properly. He and his school friends needed to rise from their seats when a teacher entered the classroom, and otherwise sit silently until called to speak. And silence meant not even coughing. I'm not sure whether my father obeyed all the time, being the prankster that he was. But, he excelled as a student and he loved to read books. He had a head for German literature, my brother Sam told me.

Then came World War I, a turning point for the Gross family and other German Jews. The years before the war were pleasant. Hatred against the Jewish people declined, and those who were not as religious as my grandfather were accepted as full-fledged members of German society. That bond strengthened when Jews were drafted into the army, with some promoted to officers.

Grandpa Feivel, however, had grave doubts about sending his sons off to war. There was a lot of discussion at home about what to do. If they were to be drafted, the sons would wear the uniform of the Austro-Hungarian Empire because it ruled the part of Poland that the Grosses had come from. The sons might have been sent to fight in Serbia. Having no strong ties to either Austria, Serbia, or Germany. Hermann and Naftalie returned to the country of their birth, Poland, and Joseph and Salomon went to Holland. Emil was too feeble to be drafted. That left Max, who was needed at home to help Feivel at the butcher shop.

In late 1915, Max was drafted into the army, and stationed not too far from home. I found a photo of him wearing his uniform among my mother's collections. He was eighteen years old then, wearing a square moustache that fitted perfectly to his gaunt, handsome face and owlish eyes. The field grey wool coat he wore looked a few sizes too big and weighted down his shoulders. His lips were sealed midway between a scowl and a smile. It was his first furlough home and the last time that he wore the uniform.

The heart-breaking scenes he witnessed in his hometown were enough to convince him to desert the army. He saw soldiers on the streets with mangled arms and legs, begging for food, crying out for help. He saw the Red Cross unload trainloads of gravely wounded soldiers at one hospital. Those sights were part of the daily grind for his sister, my Aunt Hedwig, who brought Kosher food to wounded Jewish soldiers, one of those times with her soldier-brother's help.

Max had seen enough. He fled to Holland to join his two older brothers. Max's choice was a good one; Holland was not involved in World War I and became a safe place for Max to live and to learn a trade that his big brother Joseph taught him, cutting diamonds.

Max lived in Amsterdam for the remainder of the war, almost three years, before returning to Germany in 1918. He had an opportunity to go to America with Joseph, but he chose to stay home, risking imprisonment for going AWOL, absent without leave. When Max reached Frankfurt, he walked into the arms of the law for deserting his duty as a soldier and served three months in an army prison.

My mother moved to Frankfurt just about when Max was released from prison. She worked as a saleslady in a millinery shop in the Jewish section of town and shared an apartment with an older girlfriend from the orphanage. My parents' paths did not cross until fall 1922. At the time, Germany was in economic chaos; its monetary system was in total collapse, and the streets were raging with domestic strife. But the twenty-five-year-old Max didn't seem to be bothered by the calamities unfolding before his green, cat-like eyes. Instead, he darted around capitalizing on the greed of the very rich, selling them, through his contacts in Holland, expensive jewelry, silver, gold, diamonds—all traded for sought-after US dollars.

On one of those profitable days, Max walked into a millinery store to buy a hat to go with his evening attire and was struck by the soft beauty of a young woman behind the counter, the appealing sadness of her face and her furtive glances. She was impressed by his confident bearing, standing there ramrod straight with a dark three-piece suit, shiny black shoes with spats, and his razor-clean moustache, tight curly hair, and faint smell of cologne.

As he walked around the store trying on hats, he sounded as though he was doing a soft tap dance because of the small plates fastened under the toes of his shoes. Max was putting on a show and the pretty young woman behind the counter knew it. He must have asked how he looked in the black Homburg he was about to purchase, and she would have answered with her soft smile, her dark oval eyes showing a delightful glimmer that waited for the next question she was hoping to hear, or so I imagine. Would she go out this evening for supper and drinks? And, yes, she would. Of course, my father was wearing his new hat.

I imagine my mother-to-be wearing a dark-red dress—red was her favorite color— perhaps cut above the knee, in the fashion style of that time, her hair combed tightly, and parted a bit to the side, a few strands draped over her forehead. They enjoyed each other's company I am sure, Father telling her how much he enjoyed reading Goethe and Schiller, with shy Nacha listening to his discourse and taking in the entertainment at the cabaret he took her to, observing handsome men and beautiful women slowly sipping their liquor and puffing away on their long-stemmed cigarette holders, losing themselves in the smoke-filled nightclub that filtered out the confusing and dangerous crisis that had engulfed post-war Germany.

Nacha and Max were married on 23 February 1923 at the Börneplatz synagogue. They recited their vows amid continued unrest and the country's growing hatred toward Jews, who were being blamed for Germany's economic woes.

With German desperation growing, Adolf Hitler saw an opening to influence the course Germany would take. The violence of Hitler's organization, called the National Socialist Workers' Party, frightened young Nacha. She was all too familiar with the thunderous cries of "Sieg Heil, Sieg Heil," "To Victory," and the outstretched right hand in salute of Der Führer, the leader. She even feared the sight of the Nazi flag. It was a fear she would carry the rest of her life. Nacha would often warn me, "Pass auf, die Nazis kommen." Watch out, the Nazis are coming. These were her last words to use before she died at age 86.

Throughout 1923, Nazi thugs beat up Jewish shop owners and passers-by, and looted Jewish-owned stores. The largest of these rampages took place on 7 November, the day before Hitler attempted to overthrow the government. More than 30,000 Germans stormed into the Jewish section of Berlin, smashing windows and pilfering nearly 1,000 Jewish-owned stores. These acts of violence, plus the endless barrage of anti-Semitic propaganda must have alarmed the newlyweds. The Berlin attack was reported in the 7 November 1923 issue of the daily newspaper the *Frankfurter Zeitung*.

Two days later, 9 November, news spread of Hitler's attempt to overthrow the government and begin a "national revolution." Here he was again stalking my family. This time he reared his evil head in the infamous beer hall Putsch in Munich to claim that the government in Berlin had fallen and that the army and police had rallied "around the swastika." But the revolution failed because the military didn't back him. Hitler was sentenced to five years in prison. He served less than one year and spent that time dictating his autobiography *Mein Kampf* (*My Struggle*), a chilling account of his loathing for Jews.

Hitler was released in December and two months later, February 1924, my parents, with their two-month-old son, Sam, realized Germany was no longer a place for them, and fled to Antwerp, Belgium.

In 1928, Leo was born, and eight years later I came into the world.

And four years after that, Hitler came to pay us a visit.

Chapter 7

On the Run in Northern France

On the road to Le Treport, France, 18 May 1940: My family had left the dead car in Abbeville and all our belongings in a warehouse in the coastal town of Paris-Plage, and, luckily had been picked up by a truck already brimming with refugees. The German planes pounded the coastal region, dove down again and again without mercy on the flood of frightened refugees, and emptied their unrelenting machine guns for almost the entire day. We were forced to leap from the truck into embankments dozens of times. When the rickety vehicle resumed its course, Mama, Papa, and my brothers saw dead bodies on the road, covered in blood, their relatives screaming in agony. Mama shielded me from this, nestling my face to her chest. When the strafing stopped, we rode on to Le Treport, passing through shuffling throngs of people with nowhere to go. We arrived there the evening of 18 May, hungry, tired, and trembling.

The village, used to welcoming vacationers, was teeming with people wandering in a daze looking for any place to rest, whether in the street, on a sidewalk, or at the beach. Some were gazing through the blackness of the night, hoping for some sign of rescue that would help us escape across the English Channel. No flickering lights were seen at sea, and on land the blackness of the night in a strange place was terrifying. We were beginning to lose all hope and feared being gunned down by the German war birds soaring overhead. We drew further apart from what Papa and Mama believed to be the only certain safe haven. When we were dodging the German planes in Calais, only 25 miles separated us from England's White Cliffs of Dover. In Le Treport, the distance between France and England grew to 75 miles.

Mama and Papa were undoubtedly worried sick, but they hardly showed it to their sons. Papa was busy trying to find a place for us to sleep, and Mama was comforting her sons as best she could, assuring us that we would survive this ordeal. "Hob nicht kein moiré," Don't be afraid, she said in Yiddish, a phrase she would often repeat. Still, the strain on my parents was obvious when they each lit up a cigarette and took a deep breath to calm their nerves. Papa offered his sixteen-year-old son a cigarette, as well. Sam didn't refuse, and my mother didn't grab it back from him. Of course, Sam had smoked behind his parents' back, but the offer was made too casually for them not to know that this was not his first puff. Papa was a heavy smoker, two packs a day with a few cigars in between. His fingers had turned an ugly yellow because he always smoked his cigarette down to its stub, the nicotine staining his forefinger and thumb.

I used to watch with amazement as the ashes on his cigarette lengthened while the roll of paper disintegrated. I shrunk away from him when he coughed, a punishing consequence of his habitual smoking. It was loud and rough, and sounded like he was scraping his throat. Yet, seeing him smoke that night was comforting, as if Papa having a cigarette was a sign that we could all relax.

The town's movie theater became our resting place for the night. No film would be shown. We all dozed off, me in my mother's arms, only to be startled by the terrible noises of bombs and canon shells ripping through the scenic countryside, exploding homes, setting barns on fire, killing and mutilating cattle and people.

We didn't know what to do. If we went out, we were afraid we would be blown up. And if we stayed inside, we'd all be dead, hundreds of us, if the Germans bombed the theater. The shock and fear in our faces, the muscles aching from the tension that gripped our fragile and tired bodies bottled up the screams we wanted to make. People paced nervously in the aisles while others were sitting at the edge of their seats looking like they were watching a horror movie unfold before them. The lines to the bathrooms seemed to never end as the raunchy smell became disgustingly strong. Father and others lit up cigars and cigarettes, which perfumed the air and were a welcome relief.

In ten or fifteen minutes the bombings stopped. But we were now experienced enough to know there would be a new sortie of attacks coming. Taking advantage of this recess, people streamed out of the theater to breathe fresh air, and though it smelled of burning wood, it was still fresh air compared to the stench inside. Some young men and women ran to the beach to jump in the water - with their clothes on, in most cases the only clothes that remained in their possession. And as the night began to fade, the battered refugees gazed far out to sea for a sign of hope, to see if boats were crossing the channel from England to rescue us. Nothing.

We boarded the truck again and left Le Treport at dawn on 19 May. The sound of shelling resumed as German planes pounded the channel ports, blowing up oil storage tanks, and creating an inferno that sent flames and plumes of black smoke billowing to the sky. We dove for cover many times to escape the machine-gun attacks on refugee caravans.

The Nazi troops were on the outskirts of Abbeville where we'd been two days earlier, and no more than about 25 miles from us as we headed toward Dieppe, another of the English Channel resorts, about 25 miles south of Le Treport. In Dieppe, we boarded a train for Paris. Many other refugees joined us, and when the doors opened passengers tripped over each other in a panicked rush to get on.

Sam: The train took a long time. They were already bombing Dieppe when we were taking the train to Paris. It took us twenty-four hours to get there, which is normally a trip of two, three hours. When it was dark, they couldn't have any lights. Everything was dark. The train was absolutely packed.

But that didn't deter the sympathetic conductors from squeezing latecomers through the doors. I sat on my mother's lap, my father and brothers standing nearby, holding their spots despite all the pushing and shoving going on before the train moved. As we slowly rolled away, we saw British and French soldiers rushing through the countryside toward the English Channel. German planes flew overhead, but they did not destroy the railroad tracks. Nazi Germany already smelled victory and obviously realized it would need the rail lines to transport soldiers deeper into France.

In better times, Parisians rode the same trains in the opposite direction to vacation at the beaches along the northern shore of France. The visitors were attracted to the resorts because they knew that in a mere three hours the stresses of everyday life would give way to a relaxing spirit. Our ride was much different. Not only opposite in its direction; it was a struggle to survive; it meant our very lives.

When night descended all the lights remained shut off and conductors ordered passengers not to use flashlights. I was sitting on Leo's lap, Mama having traded places to give him a break. The blackness inside the train was smothering. I had a hard time seeing my parents, even though they stood right next to me. Sensing my restlessness, Mama stroked my head and leaned over to say again, "Don't be afraid."

The car was steaming hot because it overflowed with people who were practically glued to each other, unable to move a hand to scratch an itch or cover up a cough. But we endured as the train bore us through the continuous blackout and massive air attacks against the Allied front and turned southeast toward Paris. Farmland was on either side of the tracks, and when the train stopped for short periods, some hungry passengers jumped out to pick beans, and returned to share them with the children. I was hungry enough to eat the raw vegetables. Looking out the window, Sam and other passengers saw a few scattered French troops wave their hands to signal the train to wait for them to board. "It's all over, it's all over," one soldier said, gasping for air. "We have lost the war." He collapsed.

The air strikes paved the way for the German infantry's deadly blow to the coastal area where we had been trapped for almost one week. Less than two days after we fled from Abbeville, the Nazis reduced much of that medieval city to rubble, including St. Vulfran, the remarkably magnificent fifteenth-century Gothic cathedral that earlier in the week had risen above me majestically in the dawn and provided me a moment's peace.

Chapter 8

VISITING AUNT HEDWIG IN PARIS

We entered Paris in the late afternoon of 20 May 1940. It was one of those breathless spring days, a fresh crispness in the air, cool but comfortable, a perfect day to take a stroll in the park, munch on some chestnuts. However, in spring 1940, the city was not like the lyrics in the celebrated song *April in Paris* one of my mother's favorites: "...April in Paris / Whom can I run to / What have you done to / My heart..."

Parisians were shedding tears that their beloved country would fall to Hitler, horrified to learn that France was on the verge of becoming Nazi Germany's next trophy. What would this evil man do to the French heart?

When we entered Paris, Papa called his sister, Aunt Hedwig, who lived there with her husband, Sam Katz, and their two sons, Theo and Manfred. He asked her to pick us up at the train station, the station that was crowded with refugees streaming into the capital of France. My cousin Manfred was nineteen-years-old and owned a small car. He picked us up and drove to his parents' apartment. On the way, we saw crowds around the entrances of restaurants and cafés, listening to radios with worried expressions on their faces. Some were seen loading suitcases into their vehicles. Parisians were running away from their beloved City of Lights.

"Were there any Germans when we were in Paris?" I asked Sam years later.

Sam answered, "No, but there was panic in Paris."

Public servants at the Quai d'Orsay, a vast palatial building
housing the Ministry of Foreign Affairs, tossed secret
government documents out the windows into huge bonfires
crackling with raging flames, burning not just its secrets but also
its beautiful gardens, the fire sending up billows of black smoke
that swirled overhead.

"It's so good to see that nothing happened to you," said
Aunt Hedwig, a stout woman who seemed ten feet tall to me.

"We thought you would never be able to get out of
Belgium," said Uncle Sam, a skinny man who resembled a
rumpled professor with horn-rimmed glasses.

My aunt hugged us all and repeated how relieved she was to
see us, not in the manner families are usually welcomed, not
with laughter and smiles, but with extreme concern. The
wrinkles on her forehead were so deep with worry you could
have stuck pennies into them. We let her greet us for what
seemed like forever, though we couldn't wait to take off our
clothes and wash off the smell of smoke that had covered us from
the bombings. Papa and my two brothers took baths first, and
Mama washed me before she took hers. The water on my body
was warm and comforting, especially when Mama poured it over
my head to wash my hair. Mama knew I liked that. She also
knew I wanted my hair neat and she took great care in combing
it.

Papa was excited about looking clean and refreshed. He was
very particular about his appearance. He lathered his face with a
brush borrowed from Uncle Sam and meticulously shaved his
eleven-day-old stubble. He then snipped the hair out of his nose
with a small scissor, and, pursing his lips, trimmed his
moustache with great care. I thought of the day when I would be

old enough to do the same. Mama was busy scrubbing clothes, refusing Hedwig's offer to help. She wanted to keep busy.

Later we settled into their beds for our first real rest since the invasion of Belgium. I slept through the night, while the grownups were up into the early morning of 21 May, anxiously listening to the radio, keeping track of the German march toward Paris.

Papa's brother, Hermann, lived in Limoges, in the southern region of France. That morning, Papa called him to let him know that we arrived safely in France and were at Hedwig's.

"We have no idea how long we can stay in Paris," Papa told my uncle, "and now Hedwig is afraid she'll be forced to leave."

"If you come down here," Uncle Hermann offered, "I'll help you get settled in."

"It's too dangerous for all of us to stay in one town," Papa reasoned. "If the Nazis overrun us, we'd all vanish without a trace."

There were fourteen in all, Papa and Aunt Hedwig's families, Uncle Hermann and his wife, and Emil and his wife and son.

"Have Hedwig come down to me then and you go to Bordeaux," Uncle Hermann told my father. "There's a chance you could escape into Spain."

The two oldest siblings, Joseph and Rosa, did not have to make these excruciating life and death decisions. Fearful of being arrested for dodging the draft in the First World War, Joseph, living then in Holland, did not return to Germany. He went to America, and was followed later by his wife and five children. Rosa fled to Argentina in 1933 when Germany came under Hitler's grip.

Hermann told Max that he was afraid for their brother Salomon in Holland, and their sister Mali, who was still in Germany. Their other brother, Naftalie, and his wife, went into hiding soon after the Nazis invaded Poland in September 1939, and nobody had heard from them since then.

"I tried to telephone them, but nobody answered," Hermann said. "I'm afraid, my God, I'm afraid we'll never seem them. This isn't the way it's supposed to be."

Max, on the other end of the line, lit up a cigarette and sighed deeply into the phone. "You can't give up on them. Everybody is making calls trying to reach their relatives, and the phone lines may just be too busy. You have to keep on calling."

For the next two days, 22 and 23 May, the Nazis pushed the British and French forces up against the sea in Boulogne, Calais, and Dunkirk. The Germans then shifted their focus to attack French units retreating towards Paris.

Chapter 9

FLEEING TO BORDEAUX

On 28 May, Belgium surrendered, giving Hitler control of the country of my birth. At that instant the full strength of Germany's military might turned toward France, thrusting triumphantly through its northern section, its aim to plunge a dagger into the heart of the country: Paris.

Millions of French people joined Belgians and Dutch refugees heading south. Our family, slightly recovered from the exhausting journey, resumed our own march. We left late morning on 29 May and arrived in Bordeaux early evening in the company of a train full of refugees determined to survive. We had covered a distance of some 600 miles from Antwerp.

Bordeaux, a prominent port city on the Atlantic coast in southwestern France, was already swarming with thousands of displaced people. We craved some peace after dodging the German warplanes and watching the sky turn dark from the ashes of burning villages. We stayed in a small hotel, doing nothing, just sitting and waiting, and walking around.

We were lucky to find a room. Many others slept in cars and trucks, on park benches and sidewalks, in public gardens and inside the train station. I longed for my train set to keep me amused, or for Mama to at least read a book to me or play a game. But those normal activities were all packed up in Antwerp and part of the past. Mama had little patience for me; her spirits were down, and she seemed tired of running. Sometimes she sat in a chair hunched over with an elbow resting on her leg, her chin cupped in her hand as she drifted to sleep only to startle herself awake and briefly comfort me.

The only excitement during the first few days in Bordeaux was the news from the radio. What blared out didn't make any sense to me. I heard words like Dunkirk, Hitler, Churchill, Paris, but I wasn't able to piece them together to understand what was happening. Still, the announcer's voice, trembling and urgent, and the worried look on the listeners' faces at the hotel, were enough for me to understand that bad things were going on.

The British, along with units from France and Belgium, were forced to flee to the edge of the English Channel, where we had teetered for days waiting for a miracle, for the waters to open up, for boats to sail in and rescue us. When the main forces of the Belgian army collapsed, Winston Churchill ordered Allied troops to evacuate the French shores for the British isle. The boats that we had desperately sought during our flight through the narrow strip along the English Channel were bobbing in the waters by the hundreds, evacuating Allied troops. There were so many rescue boats that if lined up straight we could have hopped from one to the next and reached England without touching water.

But if we had reached the British shore, we would not have been allowed a free pass, as I learned later. The British government in spring 1940 imprisoned some 28,000 foreign refugees suspected of being "enemy aliens" in internment camps, most of them German Jews who had fled from Nazi persecution in the 1930s. Britain did open its border for the Kindertransport (children's transport) program that brought in 10,000 Jewish children from Germany in 1938 through1939, but refused their parents permission to accompany them.

During the war, Britain was reluctant to admit Europe's Jews, insisting that its aim was not to rescue them, but to win the war as quickly as possible to save them.

The only safe path out of the Nazi stranglehold was southern France. Refugees continued to stream into Bordeaux by the tens of thousands from all over Europe, mostly from Holland, Belgium, and northern France. Bleary-eyed and ragged-looking, the new arrivals brought with them the fear and terror that we had momentarily escaped.

Other families began to think about escaping through neutral Spain and Portugal. We were a little more than 100 miles from Spain's northernmost border. Portugal was safely lodged on the edge of the Atlantic Ocean in the Iberian Peninsula and separated from an embattled France by the vast barren land of Spain. However, without a Portuguese entry visa, the Spanish government wouldn't allow Jews to pass through.

Papa's thoughts clearly lingered on his six brothers and sisters scattered throughout Europe. On 3 June, Papa heard that the Germans had bombed Paris. He rushed to call his sister. He breathed a sigh of relief when Hedwig answered the phone.

"Don't you think it's time to leave Paris?" he asked Hedwig.

"It isn't that easy," she explained. "We want to store everything we have, and go to the bank to take out our money."

"Just leave the furniture and what you can't carry in the house, and if the stuff is still there when you come back, fine. If not, then buy some new furniture." Papa's tone was not one of exasperation, but of tenderness.

"Very funny," she shot back at the family comedian.

Aunt Hedwig was a scrappy woman and held firm. She said they would wait a few more days before they made up their minds to leave. And like Papa, she was at her best when danger knocked at the door. Her husband, Sam, was the opposite, a quiet, gentle man who liked to show off his tall, lanky figure, which seemed out of place with his pudgy, wrinkled face. When danger knocked Uncle Sam's response was to calm the waters and assure with his surprisingly confident attitude that things would work out.

On 4 June, Adolf Hitler ordered the almost 1.5 million German troops along the 140-mile front stretching from Abbeville to Luxembourg to destroy France. That day, Mama, who had not set foot out of the hotel since our arrival in Bordeaux, went to the bank to exchange Belgian francs for 500 French francs, worth about 20 dollars. When she came back, Mama told Papa she heard that refugees were rushing to Spain.

"We can't stay here any longer," she pleaded. "The Nazis will soon be here. They told me it will be safe in Spain."

"It's too early to think about that," he replied indifferently. "I know what I'm doing."

"It's too dangerous to stay here," she said, her voice rising with fear.

"This is no time to get into a fight," he said, controlling his temper. "It'll upset the children."

"Sam, tell him we must go!" Mama begged.

"I think Mama is right," Sam told his father.

Sam, caught between confronting Papa and soothing Mama, stood silent, dug himself out of a spot by lighting a cigarette, and walked out of the room, signaling to his brothers to go with him. We stayed outside the hotel, which was in the center of town near the railroad station and a short distance from the Portuguese consulate. Many refugees wandered there, hinging their hopes for freedom on the man who resided inside, the Portuguese consul-general in Bordeaux, Aristedes de Sousa Mendes.

Sousa Mendes, a career diplomat in his mid-fifties and a devout Catholic, was the father of fourteen children. He cut an elegant and handsome figure, not unlike my father. Sousa Mendes was torn between his loyalty to Portugal and his compassion for the many people who, like us, were caught in a life-and-death struggle. The Portuguese government ordered him not to issue visas to Jews who had no homeland to return to, Jews who were stateless. It was an order he did not agree with, and he must have struggled with it.

At 4 A.M. on 5 June, the battle for France began as Hitler's forces raged through the French and British troops. The Germans soon smelled victory and set their sights on Paris.

Josef Goebbels, Hitler's propaganda minister, had written an ominous entry in his diary on 6 June, "We shall deal quickly with the Jews." Of course, Mother never knew of that entry. She didn't have to—her universal mistrust of people detected danger quickly. She felt something in the air and pleaded with Max to flee from the oncoming German military. He wasn't ready, ever the one to wait until he heard the signal as loud as Mother did.

By 10 June, the French had been driven back across the Seine, and the Fascist dictator of Italy, Benito Mussolini, declared war on France. His forces crossed the border to take control of the French Riviera and entered the city of Nice, the luxurious sunbathing refuge of wealthy Europeans.

Commenting on the Italians' sudden aggressive actions, Hitler snarled, "First they were too cowardly to take part. Now they are in a hurry so they can share the spoils."

Finally, all the grave news reported over the radio following 10 June began to worry Papa as he harbored second thoughts about his decision to stay in Bordeaux. He called his brother, Hermann, in Limoges, to find out whether Hedwig and her family were already there. They were not. Papa then called Hedwig, who remained calm as her brother railed at her for not having left Paris yet.

"Bist meshiga!" he barked at her in Yiddish. "You're nuts! When do you plan to go?"

"We're packing our things up," she answered.

Mama was furious that her husband seemed to worry more about his sister than us. "They can take care of themselves," Mama shouted. "The Germans will be down here soon, and we need to get out."

On 11 June even the French government moved its capital to Bordeaux before eventually settling in the town of Vichy. The next day, in a conceding gesture, the French government declared Paris an open city, meaning that it would not fight the German troops when they entered into the city. At dawn that day, Hedwig and her family squeezed into her son Manfred's little car and fled to Limoges. Everything in Hedwig's apartment remained behind. Before they left, she called Papa one more time before the phone was shut off.

"Max, we're leaving now. We will call you when we get to Limoges."

Driving to Limoges was tiresome and slow as they weaved in and out of the crowds of displaced, panicked people, stopping themselves many times as well to take cover as German planes roared over and sprayed them with machine-gun fire.

Papa was relieved his relatives were on their way. The time had come to turn his attention to the task ahead, finding a way for us to escape from France. He heard that the Portuguese counsel was starting to pass out visas specifically to Jewish people.

That same day, French leaders appealed to President Roosevelt to declare war on Germany, hoping it would raise the spirits of the French to continue the fight. France received Roosevelt's reply: "The American government is doing everything in its power to make available to the Allied governments the material they so urgently require, and our efforts to do still more are being redoubled."

Though he did not declare war, the French government wanted its countrymen to know of Roosevelt's support and asked permission to publish the statement. The president refused to give that permission. He was not ready to commit himself yet.

On the morning of 14 June, German forces marched into Paris, fulfilling Hitler's dream to take possession of the fabled City of Lights. By then, 2 million Parisians had fled, leaving about 700,000 to wake up in the morning to the sound of German loudspeakers announcing an 8:00 P.M. curfew. A thousand miles to the east, Germans began deporting a few hundred Polish citizens to a new concentration camp named Auschwitz. Auschwitz would soon carve itself a place in infamy, beginning the extermination of nearly one million Jewish men, women, and children there alone.

Papa called Hedwig in Limoges on 15 June; she had arrived the day before. The conversation was short because of the long line at the hotel's lone telephone. Many others were waiting to reach their relatives. Papa's voice was somber and conveyed the fear that brother and sister may never see each other again.

"We've made up our minds to go to Spain," my father said. "It's our only hope."

"Max, what are we going to do? It doesn't look good," Hedwig whispered, choking back her tears. "You do whatever you have to do to save your family."

"We'll get through it. All of us will." Papa had difficulty raising his solemn mood to one of hope.

On the morning of 16 June, Sousa Mendes defied his government's order and announced that he would give everyone in need a visa. The news spread like a comforting rain shower in the stifling heat of a summer's day. Thousands of Jews stampeded Sousa Mendes's office over the next few days. At first, there was a festive air to the scene as parents, their hearts pumping with joy at the thought there was an angel in their midst, assured their smiling children they would soon be safe.

But that emotion was short-lived. The next day, 17 June, the head of the French government, Marshall Henri Philippe Pétain, went on the radio to inform the French people that he was negotiating surrender with the Germans. That was the same man who led France to victory in World War 1, defeating the German army in the famous Battle of Verdun, from which my father had deserted as a young German soldier.

With the Nazis marching toward Bordeaux, Sousa Mendes worked frantically to speed up the process of granting transit visas. He delegated a few staff members to fetch passports or other identity papers from the waiting refugees, and for his secretary to rubber-stamp them as he skipped formalities and hastily scribbled his last name only.

Documents in hand, we left Bordeaux the morning of 19 June as more refugees arrived by train and car and others scurried to get out. We took a taxi and drove for more than two hours south to Hendaye, a beachhead along the Spanish-French border, hoping to escape from the ever-tightening grip of the Germans.

"You'll never make it because the Nazis are already guarding the border," the cab driver warned.

Papa ordered him to proceed anyway. We arrived in Hendaye in the late afternoon and saw thousands of frantic people pushing towards the border. Those without visas stood no chance of crossing into Spain during these few days of unrest. And seeing the Nazi secret police, the Gestapo, posted on the Spanish side, monitoring the exodus, along with the French police and Spanish border guards, frightened many Jews who did carry visas. The Gestapo had rushed down to the border to secure the Atlantic side of France and to capture Germany's best writers, artists, and musicians that opposed Hitler and who were believed headed to Spain.

Mama, more than Papa, had wanted to go to Spain but changed her mind when word spread that the French police were detaining draft-eligible men for what was left of the French army. Strangely, Papa felt relieved that we didn't reach Spain. He didn't want to leave behind Hermann and Hedwig and perhaps his other siblings hiding in Holland, Germany, and Poland. And Mama, who had argued with Papa about lingering in France too long, told him she would never sacrifice a son for her freedom.

"We must stay together as long as we can," she insisted.

"I can take care of myself," Sam said. "You go to Spain, and I'll go into hiding and meet up with you later."

"You stay with us," Papa said, offering Sam a cigarette.

Hours after we fled Bordeaux, the Germans bombed the hastily assembled new French capital, determined to extract surrender.

Four days later, on 23 June, Adolf Hitler stepped into Paris as victor to visit many of the marvelous architectural sites he had admired as an art student. After leaving Napoleon's Tomb, he said, "That was the greatest and finest moment of my life."

Chapter 10

A Farmer Hides Us in His Barn

In a desperate attempt to keep at bay the rush of panic that set in among the homeless, the International Red Cross pleaded with people hovering close to the Spanish border to board their buses to transport them into the interior of France, away from the Nazis who were about to enter the region.

Buses rolled into villages and towns, dropping off refugees at stops along the way. We were transported to Dax, northeast of Hendaye. There were reports that France would surrender in a few days and that Germany would then control the upper two-thirds of the country, including the entire Atlantic Coast down to the Spanish border. Marshall Pétain would administer the unoccupied part from Vichy in central France.

We didn't know where Dax fit in Hitler's scheme. It was one of France's top spa towns, with hot springs and mud baths, and where, according to legend, the Emperor Augustus brought his daughter Julia for a rheumatic cure. When we arrived, the bus driver got out and locked the exit doors. Confusion set in as some doubted whether we were on a Red Cross bus or on one that was not on a rescue mission but on a mission to imprison us. Papa, Sam, and other men rushed to pry open the doors, but couldn't. Some people jumped out the windows and ran in different directions, dragging their children with them, vanishing in an instant.

The driver returned about five minutes later to tell us that he had needed approval from the mayor to let us off. "I can only let families with children off the bus," he said with difficulty, explaining that Dax could only take a certain number of refugees, and that he would take the rest to other villages. These small towns did not want to be overrun by wandering Jews and essential supplies were limited. Since my parents had children, we were allowed off.

A farmer passing through town offered to hide us at his farm. Papa and Mama welcomed his generosity and offered to pay for the accommodations, which turned out to be a barn filled with bales of hay. The farmer accepted the offer, and the farmer's wife did her best to comfort us. She offered us food, typically thick potato soup, milk, and cheese. The ferocious summer heat took a toll on Mama, who suffered from hay fever. She soaked herself with buckets of water and wrapped wet towels around her neck.

"I don't know how much longer I can go on," she told Papa, barely able to gather the strength to talk. "I'm too weak to even stand up." Papa had no response. About this time I began to get a hint that this was no longer a little boy's fantasy adventure.

"When are we going home?" I asked, and all I got in return were blank stares from my parents and brothers. "I want to go home!" It may have been the only complaint I made during all that period. And sometimes, though not directly aware of it, I was the one who comforted my family, telling them not to be scared. In our interviews, Mother remembered the poise with which I behaved and seemed in awe of me whenever she talked about it. "Hob nicht kein moiré" was a Yiddish phrase I had repeated to console my family: "Don't be afraid."

"Freddy, you were such a good boy," Mama often told me. "I didn't even know you were there."

Living in a barn didn't match with what I had seen earlier in the day on the bus ride. We had ridden through one of the most striking regions of Europe: the long, lonely stretches of beaches and sand dunes, huge pine forests and sweeping curves of rolling hills, quaint brick houses with red-tiled roofs, and medieval castles that poked out from under lush-green trees, all very much different from our present accommodations.

In looking back, I would have preferred to be home listening to the rumbling but sweet sounds of the trains passing by my window. Instead, we were buried in the dry, coarse smell of hay, choking our throats and swelling our eyes. There were no prison bars to prevent us from leaving, but horrifying thoughts of Nazis in the vicinity forced us to stay inside the barn. Then, before dawn on 23 June, the farmer burst in to warn us of rumors that German tanks were rumbling through the countryside.

"You must go now," said the farmer, who feared for our lives. "We think the Germans will be taking over this stretch of land."

Since we were sleeping in our clothes, we just shook off the hay that stuck on us and trudged through the woods towards what would become the boundary line that separated German-controlled France from the territory to be administered by the Vichy government.

The night before, 22 June, at precisely ten minutes to seven, France signed the surrender agreement granting Germany control over 60 percent of France. France's Vichy government would be established in the lower portion of the country, which would be referred to as the unoccupied or free zone.

By daybreak we crossed into the unoccupied zone. International Red Cross buses were waiting on the roads for the hordes of refugees to appear from beneath the morning mist that covered the region. Mixed in with the crowd were tattered French troops, slogging in boots that were peeling off their weary feet. My family and I boarded a bus that transported us to Pau, a city in the foothills of the rugged Pyrénées Mountains that separated France from Spain.

Sam: We went to Pau and they took us to a school. There were loads of people coming into Pau, and all the hotel rooms were taken when we got there.

Leo: People were sleeping in the street, and hanging around the square.

Where did we sleep?

Sam: In a school.

Leo: Not in the school, in the square.

Sam: It was in a school. There was no place to go, and we were sleeping in a school auditorium. They said this is where you can sleep. We slept on straw.

Who is "they?"

Sam: People in the street.

Chapter 11

FRANCE COLLABORATES WITH HITLER

Mama said in Pau, "Thank God, we are here." Mama and Papa were relieved that we were finally in seemingly friendly territory.

Pau is the capital of the Basses-Pyrénées (now Atlantique-Pyrénées) region. France is carved into separate regions, or departments similar to states in America, each headed by a chief executive called the prefect, who is equivalent to a US governor, though appointed by the department's legislative body.

The Pyrénées loom high above Pau. When we arrived, we acted more like tourists than refugees, walking along the Boulevard des Pyrénées, which was lined with palm trees, with one end reaching to a massive structure that contained a medieval fortress and a Renaissance palace. The refugees lingered in a lush square, Place Royale, where trees shaded benches under a brilliant azure sky.

The school where we slept lay on a side street off the boulevard. The school's tiny gym overflowed with people. I couldn't stand to hear the weeping, or to look at the scared faces or to smell the stench of body odor. Each morning, we rose before the students came to school and were served bread and water for breakfast and then left to roam the streets, or hang around the square. Breathing the fresh morning air and bathing our faces in the mountain breezes were a welcome relief.

Still, the refugees were always on guard, darting their eyes at the ever-present police and the suspicious looking villagers. My parents and others did not really know how safe the unoccupied zone was as rumors spread of the French government starting to cooperate with the Germans in making life miserable for the Jews. I don't know how long we stayed in Pau; all I know is that we were still there on 27 June. According to her identification card, that's when Mama went to a branch office of the Bank of France and exchanged 3,000 Belgian francs for French francs.

A day or two later, the French police burst into the gym and ordered all one hundred of us to board school buses.

Mama: They said we didn't have a place to sleep. There were so many people here. So, they said they would bring us to a place to sleep. It turned out to be a camp.

What was the name of the camp?

Mama: I don't know that either anymore. You have to ask Sam. He would know.

Who brought us to this camp?

Mama: The French police. It was a French camp and we were there with a lot of people. You were almost four years old.

So they captured us?

Sam: No, no, no, no, no. They said they're going to bring us someplace because they didn't know what to do, and we didn't know what they were doing.

Leo: They said they prepared villas for us, telling us there were lots of refugees from Belgium in Pau and that the mayor didn't want us to sleep on the streets or in the gym. "We will send you to small villages around Pau," we were told, and they sent us instead to a concentration camp called Gurs.

Chapter 12

Taken to Gurs Concentration Camp

About 27–28 June 1940. The school buses pulled up to a massive rectangular compound ringed by barbed wire and guarded by French Army reserves. Distance from Pau to Gurs: 35 miles.

Leo: All of a sudden we saw Gurs.

Sam: We got frightened.

Leo: Women were apart. Men were apart. It was terrible. It was scary.

Sam: Very scary.

Mama: We were frightened the Germans would come in and that we would never get out.

As soon as the gates opened, guards shouted for the women and children to rush to one side and for the men to race to the other. The guards, female on our side, shoved my mother and I past a barbed wire fence, barking at us to go directly to a registration center.

Papa and my brothers went through another entrance on the other side of a long central alley separating the men from the women. Two 8-foot-high barbed wire fences 15 feet apart stretched almost a mile from one end to the opposite end of the alley, with armed guards patrolling within the partition. We were horrified at the thought of never seeing each other again. There was no moment for goodbyes, and in an instant we disappeared from each other's view.

The line for the registration desk snaked around the building, old women trembling with fear, mothers and children crying, eyes bulging with horror. Mama's hand firmly gripped mine, her far-off expression suggesting that this seemed like a bad dream. As we reached the front of the line, Mama's dream-like look turned into anger, the kind she was able to flash in a moment in a fight with Papa.

"We are being treated like animals," she complained, knifing her voice into the soldier behind the desk. "Why are we here in the first place?" she demanded. "We've done nothing wrong."

"What did she say?" the soldier, not understanding German, asked a woman prisoner who interpreted for him.

"She said animals are treated better than us," the woman replied in the same tone as my mother's.

"Don't worry," the reservist answered with a sheepish, guilty voice. "We're only going to ask you a few questions and assign you to a block. We are not going to do anything to you. The French are in control here."

"Is the Gestapo here?"

"No, they will *never* be here," the soldier assured her in a way that did not hide his own hatred of the Nazis.

Mama relaxed her grip, a hint that the man was calming her fears.

"What's your name?" he asked, as he handed her paper and pencil to write down the information.

"Nacha Gross."

"Where were you born and when?" was the next question.

"Pabiance, Poland, January 28, 1903."

"Last place of residence?"

"Antwerp, Belgium."

"How did you get here?"

"The Nazis drove us out of our home."

Female guards took the women and children to their barracks, passing through yet another barbed wire fence to reach the assigned block. Mama was shaken by what she saw. Our barrack was made out of wood, as were all the barracks, and seemed on the verge of collapsing, as flimsy as a house of cards. Mama touched the walls gently and found them damp from the recent rain. "Come, sit with us," a woman invited Mama in Spanish, gesturing her to sit on the ground, which was still drying out from a weeklong downpour.

"Hello," she said to me kindly.

"Freddy, come here." Mama was suspicious.

I plopped down next to my mother and watched the woman produce a comb and gently stroke Mama's disheveled hair. Mama began to cry, a quiet cry, and the tears flowed down her face as she took me in her arms and struggled to bury her fright.

"Mama, hob nicht kein moiré," I said to her in Yiddish. Mama, don't be afraid.

We went into the barrack and saw the light from outside sneak in through the walls and ceilings. The sun was dazzling, knifing sharp beams of light through the cracks, illuminating dust that danced within its rays. The windowpanes were barely visible to me since they were almost touching the edge of the ceiling. The wooden floor was covered with straw, which was thinned down by the trampling of all the pairs of feet that were living here. There were no real beds—only wooden beds with straw—and no furniture. Luggage was used for chairs and tables.

Papa and my two brothers were submitted to the same routine.

"What is your name?"

"Markus Gross." Papa answered with his given name even though he had preferred to be called Max since his days as a teenager. He felt it had a greater ring of authority.

"Where and when were you born?"

"Frankfurt, Germany, September 20, 1897."

"Where was your last place of residence?"

"Antwerp, Belgium."

Papa asked no questions, but simply followed orders and closely guarded the few packs of cigarettes he had purchased in Pau and the family's cash. Meanwhile, Mama hid the diamonds in a silk paper pouch tucked in her girdle. Luckily, the guards did not frisk my parents. Papa and my brothers were also located in a block housing mostly Spanish refugees.

The Spaniards, mostly socialists and communists, had been engaged in a civil war with General Franco that began in July 1936. The bloody battle ended on 1 April 1939 with Franco achieving victory with a little bit of help from Hitler, who supplied him with military aid.

Formerly used for military maneuvers, the camp at Gurs was located on the foothills of the Pyrénées, a mere 40 miles from the Spanish border. It opened on 25 April 1939 and became the home of almost 20,000 Spanish refugees of the nearly 100,000 that fled from the civil war and roamed through France's southern countryside. To please the villagers who bristled at this intrusion in their lives, France set up pockets of internment camp along its border with Spain, among them Gurs, where many were put to work to complete building the complex of 428 barracks—382 for refugees, and 46 for the troops. These temporary quarters were built to last only a few months.

By summer 1940, the French had liberated most of the Spanish captives and turned Gurs into a concentration camp for

Jews who had fled from Belgium, Holland, Austria, and Germany.

Gurs was the largest of the six major concentration camps established in the unoccupied zone. It covered an area of 200 acres, 1 1/4 miles long and 1,100 feet wide. The harsh, unproductive land, with not even a tree on it, nor a blade of healthy grass, was grounded in the most humid section of France.

The week before we were deported to Gurs, it had rained almost every day, turning the earth into a pool of slimy, thick mud so deep that anybody who stepped outside the barracks got sucked in knee-deep mud. We arrived just as it stopped raining; the fresh air and cool breezes coming from the mountains were soothing. It was the kind of day Mama would have taken me to the neighborhood park and let me play in the sandbox. At Gurs there was no sandbox, only mud and fear.

Our block consisted of 24 barracks housing about 1,500 prisoners. There were thirteen blocks, labeled A through M. The blocks held as many buildings as ours, with barbed wire looped around each from top to bottom. Each block was so similar to the next that neither Mama nor I remember in which block we were kept.

Keeping clean was the hardest, and, like a dog, I'd relieve myself around the perimeter of the barrack, rather than come near the block's half-opened, stench-filled outhouses. The toilets were about six feet off the ground and propped up by thick boards. Prisoners had to climb up crumbling wooden steps without handrails and squat over a hole packed with a metal drum to catch the feces. Mama was among the many women who gagged and threw up from the dreadful smell and the sight of bugs buzzing around.

Nights were tough on me because nobody was allowed outside the barracks then. I remember the times I had to urinate in the worst way, but I didn't want to wake Mama, nor go outside alone in the dark. I used the bed of straw I slept on to empty my bladder and laid down to go to bed, soaking the little overcoat I had worn since leaving Antwerp.

Mama washed my clothes and me in a huge wooden water trough, similar to what farm animals drink from. The trough, just outside the living quarters, contained eight sinks and cold water only. Mama had to scramble with other women to get to one in the morning to wash the clothes the children peed in. And because, unlike rain, there was a shortage of water, basins could only be used from seven to eleven o'clock in the morning, and from two to five o'clock in the afternoon.

Near the block's entrance was a barrack reserved for warm showers in stalls that were not exactly arranged for privacy. Mama cringed when she went into the showers, having no choice but to strip at the water basin—and lose whatever scrap of dignity remained. She trudged on her tiptoes to avoid the slime that caked the floor of the shed, slime that wallowed in a pool of water that sported bobbing balls of fallen hair from fellow prisoners and gooey piles of discarded soap.

Fleas, bedbugs, lice, and rats were among our daily guests, and they feasted on us as if we were leftover dinner. I had insect bites all over my legs, which Mama treated with mud, watering the ground hardened by the sun's rays to manufacture my medicine.

The bugs seemed to have more to eat than we had. Our meals were prepared in a small shed that was called a kitchen. Soup, chickpeas, and occasionally meat were cooked in huge kettles. The menu for the day consisted mainly of chickpeas and a piece of hard bread. In the evenings we ate a small bowl of soup and sometimes a tiny portion of meat. The starvation and unsanitary conditions under which we lived began to take its toll, as hundreds of prisoners, most of them elderly, died of typhoid and severe diarrhea.

Our world had closed in, and the boundaries of our existence shrunk to only 66 feet long, 16 feet wide, and 7 feet high. We shared this tiny space with 50 other women and children. The territory of our existence outdoors was limited to the length of a football field and a mere 175 feet in width, the size of our block.

What was it like to be a prisoner?

Sam: The Spanish people were very nice to us.

Leo: Oh, very nice. There were Gypsies there, too.

I'm talking about the authorities.

Leo: We didn't see much of them. We saw a few Germans once. They came in for inspections. German officers, the SS.

In their uniforms?

Leo: That's right. They visited the camp, and that's all.

Mama: We were frightened that we would be taken away by the Germans because we couldn't get out of the camp.

The site of the SS alarmed my mother. She desperately wanted to talk to my father, but inmates were forbidden to speak through the barbed wires. She sprinted along the fence that divided us from Papa and my brothers, hoping that she could get a glimpse, if only to know that they were still there. My mother was not alone. Some of the other women made an effort to speak to their male relatives, but the sentries inside the central alley poked their rifles through the twisted metal forcing us to back off. I often heard people shouting words to the guards in languages that I didn't understand.

Commander Davergne came to the barracks to calm the women's fears. His uniform was splattered with sweat from the sticky, humid heat, and the commander was asked again and again what the Gestapo would do with us. He replied, "France is taking full responsibility for your safety."

The German officers were ordered to comb through the more than fifty concentration camps in the southern region to weed out refugees who fussed about Hitler's treachery, many of them German politicians and writers, some Jewish, some not. They didn't find any, but when they entered Gurs in vehicles and trucks on 30 June, they were also greeted with shouts of Heil Hitler. The voices belonged to hundreds of German-born women imprisoned by the French as enemy aliens before the Nazi invasion. The Gestapo ordered their release, and the first batch of departing German women, rejected by the non-German inmates during their stay, yelled to us: "You wait. Now it's our turn. We'll soon come back for you." The Gestapo trucks came twice to take all 600 Nazi internees home.

We wanted to go home, too. When France surrendered on 22 June, the French soldiers guarding the camp had no idea what would happen to them since Hitler ordered their army to disband. The French were confused, and shocked by their country's defeat. Worried that they might themselves become prisoners, the soldiers abandoned Gurs and made it possible for thousands of refugees to follow them. Some didn't want to escape because they were more afraid of what was lurking in the foothills of the Pyrénées than within their barbed wire world.

Ministers that were known to hate Jews led the new Vichy government. Though it hadn't yet issued anti-Semitic laws, the naming of these officials sent a signal to the regional prefects and village mayors to get tough with Jews who had no roof over their heads. With an image of the stiff, upright Nazis marching into the camp, Mama feared the French would hand us over along with the other persecuted Jews. And at four years old, I was one of them, one of the hated.

Sometime after the Nazis left Gurs, Mama secured a pass to cross into the men's unit to talk to Papa. Papa told her of a plan to escape. He had learned that when the guards changed at the front gate there was a lapse when the gate appeared unwatched. The question became whom to send. Leo was too young, and Papa thought leaving his wife and three sons in the camp was too risky. Sam, at sixteen years old, became the only option.

When the day arrived, Papa gave Sam his last pack of cigarettes. "Don't forget to come back for us." Papa knew he would get a laugh from my solemn-faced brother.

Sam was the image of coolness, as he walked a little over a third of a mile to the camp hospital, a group of structures framed by loose sheets of aluminum. As he approached the grounds of the hospital, he saw the front gate unguarded, and maintained his slow, casual stride so as not to draw any attention as he simply walked out. His mission was to reach Pau, the seat of the prefecture. But, first he went into Orin not far from the camp. Orin was a speck of a town not known for anything much but a bar and restaurant in the small square and a deserted, haunted-looking castle.

Sam: It was still the beginning of the war. It wasn't more than the end of June, beginning of July, maybe. We were hearing that the Germans kept advancing and somehow I escaped from the camp and went to the prefecture.

When you escaped, was it in the middle of the day, in the night?

Sam: It was during the day. I said to the guard I was going to the infirmary. I didn't feel well. The infirmary was in front of the camp. Then I just walked out. They didn't notice it, in bright daylight. I walked a little bit on the road and then hitchhiked.

By yourself?

Sam: Yeh.

And you were 16 and a half years old?

Sam: 16 or 15.

Why did you risk coming back? Why didn't you just take off? You were free now.

Sam: Why should I take off? Listen, the parents were there, the brothers were there. That's why I went to the prefect.

But it wasn't that simple. Derring-do, luck, and timing combined to set the scene for the first in a series of my family's escapes made on our perilous tour of France.

Mama: Somebody said that if you have an apartment here in the village, then you can get out of the camp. So Sam went into the city. And we were afraid about it. He was just a young boy. He was looking for a room at a farm. The people there were very nice to him. Sam then had to go to Pau and say we had a room.

What was the name of the village?

Mama: I don't remember. Sam remembers.

What did you tell the prefect?

Sam: I told him my parents and brothers are in the camp for no reason. So, he took pity on me and gave me a laissez-passer, [a document allowing the family's release].

So you went back to Gurs. Who did you give the laissez-passer to?

Sam: In the Gurs office, and they called Father and Leo. They called you and Mother, and we left. We went to Orin.

How did we leave?

Sam: In an army truck. They dropped us off in Orin and we stayed with the Kurz and Schmalz families. [They were Father's relatives, who apparently used the same escape route as did thousands of other refugees from the northern countries invaded by Germany.]

How did we know they were there?

Sam: That's a good question.... I knew...I knew because on the way to Pau, I stopped off there and met them there. In Orin, in that little village.

How long were you gone?

Sam: I was overnight there and in Pau about two days.

Ten years after interviewing Sam, I discovered how Sam knew to go to Orin. In 2001, I acquired a video of our cousin Leo Schmalz, recounting his wartime experiences to his children: "Waiting for a car to pick me up, there were buses going in the other direction, and I heard somebody yell 'Leo, Leo, Leo.' It turned out to be my mother's cousin, Max Gross. I ran after the bus and he yells at me they're going to Gurs."

Apparently, while riding on the school bus from Pau toward the Gurs concentration camp, Papa recognized a hitchhiker as his cousin Leo. Young Leo happened to be thumbing a ride to Oloron-Sainte-Marie. I called Sam minutes later.

Once in Orin, Sam wandered around town hoping his cousin Leo was still there. He was afraid to ask if anybody had seen him, thinking that Leo could have been hiding from the townsfolk. It was late afternoon when he saw our cousin wandering into town. Sam knew Leo from family gatherings in Belgium and immediately recognized the blond-haired youth with a boxer's features.

Leo and his family had lived in Brussels, the capital of Belgium, when war broke out. They were originally from Berlin and fled after witnessing their synagogue burn to the ground on the Night of Broken Glass.

"Where are your parents and brothers?" Leo asked.

"They're still in Gurs," Sam replied, anxious to devise a way to save their lives. "I've got to get them out, but I don't know how. Maybe you can help."

Leo introduced him to Orin's Mayor Rossi, who owned the village bar and restaurant, a dark and dingy place with paper-thin wooden chairs and tables. The village farmers gathered for an afternoon drink when Sam and his cousin Leo entered. Rossi sat at a table in the far corner where he had a clear view of the entrance. He was talking to a customer.

He just glanced at the two boys, waved his hand at Leo and continued his conversation. Leo Schmalz knew the mayor well because he had given his family permission to stay in Orin when they were dropped off by one of the International Red Cross buses ferrying homeless Jews away from the incoming German troops. The two teenagers walked to his table.

"We need to talk to you," Leo said urgently.

The mayor excused himself and the threesome moved apart from the regulars.

"This is my cousin Sam Gross," Leo began. "He just escaped from Gurs. His parents and two younger brothers are there now, and he wants to know how he can get them out."

"If he has a place to board, I can help," the mayor responded slowly, part of his fingers disappearing into his thick white beard, scratching, as he ruminated on what he could in actuality do to assist.

"What if they stayed with us?" Leo asked.

"I can try, but it's up to the prefect to release your family from Gurs," the mayor answered. "I'll write a letter to the prefect telling him you have found some room in Orin."

Unfortunately, Sam had to wait for the mayor's daughter to come home from school. Rossi could neither read nor write, and he depended on his teenage daughter for his correspondence.

Sam spent the night with cousin Leo and his family before departing the next morning for Pau, about 20 miles east of Orin, getting a ride from a villager.

With letter in hand, Sam simply walked into the office of the prefect, Angelo Chiappe, a rotund and loudmouthed man. After explaining how he got to his office, Sam stretched his hand out toward the prefect to offer the letter to Chiappe. "This is from the mayor of Orin for you, saying we could live in his town," Sam stated.

The silence stretched as the prefect read the letter.

"So you escaped from Gurs," the prefect said in a slow, alarming voice. "What makes you think I can save you and your family?" his voice rising. "I can send you back and order the commandant to put you in with the undesirables."

"We have done nothing wrong," Sam said softly, standing firmly in front of Chiappe.

The prefect mulled over what to do with this scruffy teenager. "I will give you a laissez-passer," the prefect said eventually, handing Sam a document "allowing" the family to "pass" through the barbed wire gates of Gurs. They parted with a firm handshake.

A few days later, on 8 July, Chiappe issued an order that was pinned on the walls of town halls throughout the region he governed, "All ex-internees of Camp Gurs must leave the department of Basses-Pyrénées within twenty-four hours, or face internment again." His order, which targeted mainly women, tightened the grip on the flow of refugees departing from Gurs, since he didn't want any of them wandering around. So, why was he so lenient with Sam?

Decades later, I would discover another piece of the puzzle on the Internet. A French Web site called "Mémoire Juive et Éducation" ("Jewish Memory and Education") noted Angelo Chiappe in a list of more than 800 Nazis and their collaborators who scorched the French earth with their deadly orders. In a one-paragraph summary, the site simply mentioned that Chiappe eventually served as prefect of Orléans, south of Paris. There, in 1942, Chiappe ordered the arrest and deportation of 3,000-4,000 Jews to the Polish killing camps. In August 1944, soon after American troops liberated France from the Nazis, Chiappe was arrested, transferred to a prison in Nimes, in southeastern France, where he was condemned to death. The prefect who had freed us from Gurs was executed on 23 January 1945.

To the Jews of Orléans, Chiappe was their death sentence. Why did he save our lives? Why didn't he intervene to save the others? How could someone be human and animal, good and evil? Did he simply follow orders as many Nazis and their

French collaborators claimed they did? I brood over these questions and feel ashamed that such a man would save me from the jaws of death, guilty that I was still alive. It was Thanksgiving 2001, midnight New York time, six o'clock in the morning in Paris, that I e-mailed the Holocaust historian who ran the Web site, Dominique Natanson, a French college professor, to find out whether he had the answers.

Natanson responded by e-mail: "Angelo Chiappe was a member of a well-known French family of the far right. The moment when the prefect Angelo Chiappe intervened on behalf of your family (the summer of 1940 if I have understood correctly), was a time when the anti-Semitic politics of Vichy were only just being sketched out: the Statute of the Jews had not yet been established. It was also a time of great disorder in the administrative authority, with a large number of Jews in the south needing to be placed where there was room. Having Jews leave the Gurs camp didn't pose a problem if they had a place to stay. The policy of extermination, of giving up Jews of the Free Zone to the Nazis was not yet in place. When he took over his duties in Orléans, however, he zealously carried out the policy of arrests and deportation."

And so, what did this mean? Had he saved us because he respected Sam's bravado? Had he saved us because it was not yet his order to do otherwise? Had it been a bit of both? I know the actions of the man only. I will never know the mind behind them.

With that precious laissez-passer document in hand, Sam hitchhiked from Pau back to Gurs, picked up for the trip by two French Army officers in a jeep who were fleeing from the Nazi zone.

Sam: I saw Father running to me when I got back into the camp. I held up the papers for him to see.

Worried about Sam's absence for almost three days, Papa ran towards him, stopped by the barbed wire fence that enclosed the barracks. Sam went to the commandant's office first to show him the laissez-passer. The commandant, exhausted from overseeing this huge mud-hole of a camp, didn't even ask how Sam got the document. It really didn't matter because the commandant had to follow the orders of the prefect, who was his boss.

"We have a place to stay in Orin," Sam told the commandant as he reviewed the papers, including a copy of the letter from the mayor.

The weary camp chief summoned guards to fetch my mother and me, and my father and Leo. I recall sitting on the barren ground outside the officer's wooden-structured compound. My mother was beside me, looking, as I did, at the rifle-toting sentries patrolling the area. An army truck pulled up near us. My eyes were fixed on the guards and the truck, which, Mama said, would take us away from Gurs.

I started fidgeting as the minutes ticked by slowly. Mama sensed my uneasiness. "We're leaving soon," she said.

In the early afternoon light, the clouds were looming over the mountains, and a chill was in the air that seemed to get colder as time went by. Staring at the truck, doubt exceeded my hope of ever boarding it. I felt we were waiting for hours when suddenly the commandant bellowed out our name: "Gross!"

That sharp roar sounded at first threatening, but turned into a joyful, climactic ending. We were now free.

Were other people on the truck?

Sam: No.

The fact that you escaped from the camp and came back—if that had not happened...?

Sam: Who knows? We might have been deported to up north because some people from Gurs never got out and were deported to the north, and from the north, who knows, to Poland?

Chapter 13

HIDING IN AN ABANDONED CASTLE

That 4-mile ride from Gurs to Orin may have marked the happiest day of my life, as the huge complex of barracks faded from view. Camp Gurs became a distant memory in a very short time for a little boy who just wanted something good to eat and to be tucked into a clean, warm bed.

On our way to the village of Orin, I fell into Mama's lap like a lump of potatoes. I was still wearing the same clothes I had worn when we fled Belgium. It was now about 10 July 1940, three months short of my fourth birthday.

"Freddy, we're here." Mama's voice was intended less as an announcement than a statement of relief that we were captives no longer.

It felt like I was back home in Antwerp as I walked on Orin's cobblestone streets, careful not to get my small feet twisted in the creases between the stones. Mayor Rossi was standing outside the town hall, where the truck pulled up to let us out. The light drizzle coated the streets with a polished shine, unlike the mud puddles at Gurs.

The mayor checked my parents' ID cards, and invited our family to his restaurant as his guest. Cousin Leo accompanied us. The mayor poured wine for Papa and Mama, my brothers, and a few drops for me, offering a toast to celebrate our safe arrival. I felt grownup, drinking wine with strangers. I downed the wine like a glass of water. I was thirsty.

"Freddy, not so fast," Mama chided.

I don't remember what we ate, but it had to be better than the food at Gurs. We devoured our meals unashamedly.

"You can stay here under our protection," the mayor informed Papa and Mama. "I don't know how long we'll be able to do that. You're never sure what's going to happen. The Nazis may not be in control of this area, but the Gestapo is everywhere looking for suspicious characters. I'll let you know when it's no longer safe to be here."

"You're very kind to help us. We will do whatever you ask us to do," said Mama, almost begging him not to tell on us, and almost not believing him, perhaps not trusting him to hold his word, always on guard, wary of being hurt.

Leo's family stayed in an abandoned castle in Orin. They had been there for a few weeks when we arrived. "It had all kinds of rooms, a fireplace with a flue that was completely plugged up," recalled Leo's sister Edith, who was twelve years old when we came to stay. "We used it for cooking, but the smoke would always come down," she said.

My parents and relatives pooled their money to buy bed sheets, pillows, and blankets and went almost daily to the butcher to buy fresh meat, though that became scarcer by the day because nobody dared to deliver food to the town and take a chance at getting captured by the Nazis, who were stealing it from the citizenry. A relative of the Schmalzes did the cooking, though not to everyone's liking.

Cousin Doriane Kurz: She was awful. When she cooked, the whole place filled with smoke and covered the meat with soot. We could hardly breathe.

Edith: The fireplace was huge and had a big hook where you hung the kettle to cook the food. The castle had enough rooms for three families, and a small yard. I remember playing in the yard. It wasn't exactly Versailles.

Childhood has its ups and downs and the contrast between living in a concentration camp and then in a castle underscored that. When Doriane first talked with me about the castle decades later, it drummed up images of medieval times, of ancient swords and suits of armor everywhere, and long, winding stairs to the towers overlooking the kingdom below. Doriane and Edith shook me back to reality with their descriptions. The yard we played in was covered with weeds. The castle's outer walls looked shabby, and in some areas there were gaping holes, as if artillery shells had previously rammed through the walls. The castle seemed to have relinquished its duties a long time ago and didn't want to be disturbed. Still, I must have had a good time staying there, as did my brothers and cousins, who most likely went exploring for hidden treasures. But the fantasy was cut short: after only a few days the mayor barged in to tell us that we had to evacuate the area immediately.

"The people are starting to speak out against the Jews, blaming you for losing the war and the shortage of food," he told us. "I've made arrangements for you to go to Oloron. There, you can catch a train to Toulouse."

On or about 13 July, we vacated the castle, carrying only blankets, resuming the journey to avoid the Vichy plan to intern displaced Jews. Eleven people from the three families packed into an oxcart and traveled south to Oloron-Ste. Marie, a 5-mile ride through the back roads to avoid the Gestapo and the French police.

Leo: It was a bit of a bumpy trip. It was fun, but crowded, with so many people in the wagon.

It was almost like a hayride. My brothers and cousins sang to pass the time. We enjoyed this rare, lighthearted moment. Mama even volunteered a faint smile. Papa caught the spirit, singing along boisterously and bouncing me up and down on his knees.

Up north, the war continued. Germany and Great Britain were locked in a battle that pitted Churchill against Hitler. On 10 July 1940, the Battle of Britain began as did Hitler's dream to set foot on England, which had been preparing for just such an invasion, ringing its shores and the city of London with thousands of anti-aircraft guns.

The station in Oloron was jammed with refugees waiting for the next train to Toulouse. Mama and Papa were anxious to flee because of growing anti-Jewish feelings among the townspeople, some of whom jeered and spat at us as we rode off.

"Go back where you came from, you dirty Jew," they shouted. "You lost the war for us. You're stealing food from our children."

Their faces were twisted in hatred, their mouths spewing and their clenched fists shaking. I pressed close to Mama and closed my eyes. The police stood by in silence, working the crowd with plainclothes Gestapo, who were slowly roving the crowd with their eyes, searching for well-known German citizens on Hitler's list who had opposed his dictatorship.

Our three families purchased tickets for the next train to Toulouse, about 120 miles northeast of Oloron and 70 miles from the Spanish border. Toulouse brimmed with Jewish refugees who had fled from the German-occupied zone. Thousands were lining up to get Portuguese and Spanish visas to leave France. Papa and Mama already had their identification cards stamped by the Portuguese counsel in Bordeaux, but couldn't get a Spanish transit visa to travel through the country unless they showed a passport from their native country, which was Poland. The Schmalzes, showing legitimate Polish passports, were able to get visas for both countries, and crossed the border into Spain, traveling by train to Portugal, the first leg of their long journey to America.

Leo Schmalz took a huge gamble in approaching the Spanish border. "We were told that the Germans insisted that the Spaniards not allow Jewish men of military age to go through Spain," he recounted to his family.

The family lived in Lisbon until January 1942 when the "International Police" expelled them from Portugal. "The police asked why we were still in Portugal," recalled Edith, Leo Schmalz's younger sister. "Our reason for staying is that we had no place else to go." That wasn't a sufficient reason for this secret police unit, which was used by the Portuguese dictatorship to expel "undesirable" refugees.

What would the family do now? "We were promised a visa to go to the United States, but the American government wanted to delay these things as much as possible, so they changed the quota regulations," Edith explained. "My brother and I couldn't go because the German quota was closed, and my parents couldn't go because the Polish quota was closed. Anyway we couldn't go, and then there was Pearl Harbor and nobody could go.

The quota set specific limits on the number of people who could emigrate in any given year from any foreign country, and eligibility was based on one's country of birth. But when the United States entered World War II in December 1941, the State Department, responsible for setting immigration policies, closed its door to Polish and German Jews fleeing from Nazi persecution.

According to the US Holocaust Memorial Museum, "Refugees with 'close relatives' living in German-occupied territory were denied entry to the US, ostensibly out of fear that they could be blackmailed into working as agents for Germany. By 1941 these policies had effectively prevented most refugees from immigrating to the United States."

Forced to exit Portugal, blocked entrance to the US, where would the Schmalz family go? Luck, that necessary strand for survival, intervened in a shadow way. "We couldn't stay in Lisbon much longer, but there were a number of things for sale, including the Cuban visa."

Paying their way toward freedom, Edith, her brother and parents arrived by boat in Havana soon after they were told to leave Portugal. The family lived in Cuba until June 1946 when the long-awaited American visa was issued.

The Gross and Kurz families decided to stay in France rather than risk taking the dangerous passage to Portugal with Edith and her family. That decision nearly cost our lives, for we had nowhere else to go.

We had nowhere to go. The surrounding countries, except for Switzerland, were in enemy hands. The Nazis controlled Belgium, Luxembourg, and France; Italy was their ally. Switzerland, which supposedly took no side in the war, had set up obstacles to prevent Jews from crossing its border. The Swiss have had a shadowy history concerning Jews trying to find refuge in their country. Many Jews began to flee Germany and Nazi-controlled Austria in spring 1938 and looked toward Switzerland, which bordered the two countries, for freedom. Alarmed they would be flooded with Jewish refugees, the Swiss reinforced its borders and required entry visas, systematically denying them. We were trapped.

Chapter 14

VICHY FRANCE'S ANTI-JEWISH LAWS

I don't know what crossed Papa's mind when he decided not to risk an escape to Spain. When I mentioned to a survivor of the Nazi Holocaust that we wound up instead in Toulouse, he asked in despair, "You didn't go to Spain?"

"No, we didn't," I replied, wondering to myself why not, and thinking that if we did, it would have been the end of my story. We went instead to Nice.

"Why did you go to Nice?" His response made me feel that Papa had let us down. I thought, how could a teenager, Leo Schmalz, save his family from hardships and terrors like the ones that would descend on me later and my streetwise father couldn't, or wouldn't. Sure, we lacked a final destination, but Papa could have at least given the same effort Leo did to find one. Papa could have contacted his wealthy cousins in New York to help us reach America. Instead, we took a train to Marseille after spending only a week in Toulouse.

We arrived in Marseille on 18 July and found a hotel on Boulevard Dugommie, walking distance from the harbor. We were lucky to find lodgings at all since most of the hotels were full. Thousands of other refugees had been turned away and so were forced to stay in schools or even small internment centers or lodgings that were guarded by the French police.

We went to Marseille for no other reason perhaps than to follow the crowd. All the refugees, not just my family, all of us, were like boats at the mercy of a storm, letting the rushing waves set our course. We remained in Marseille for nearly three months, our journey's longest rest period since the bombing of Antwerp on 10 May.

So far we had journeyed nearly 1,200 miles since departing Antwerp. In that time we had been two days in La Panne, the lush Belgian seaside resort where we came under fire from the German fighter planes. Then we crossed into France, sleeping overnight at an inn in the medieval city of Abbeville, fleeing from there at dawn to stay a step ahead of the German army's lightning advance to the coast. We found refuge at a movie theater in Le Treport, another seaside resort, and the following day reached Dieppe and boarded an overcrowded train that took us to Paris. There we stayed for nine days with Aunt Hedwig, and hearing reports that the German troops had crossed into France, we fled southward to Bordeaux by train on 29 May. We stayed in a little hotel there until 19 June when we heard that the Germans were advancing deeper into the south of France. Again, we found refuge in a small village, Dax, where a farmer allowed us to hide in his barn. But we fled four days later to Pau, sleeping in a school gym, before the French police transported us to Camp Gurs around 27 June. After less than two weeks, my oldest brother, Sam, escaped from the camp and returned with documents authorizing our release. For the moment though, we were in Marseille.

I remember Marseille, especially the hotel overflowing with refugees. My family crowded into a small room with a queen-sized bed that looked like it stood on stilts. The mattress stood about 3 feet off the ground and was covered with a tattered quilt screaming with colors that didn't match. My brothers and I slept on the floor with no blankets to warm us against the chilling breeze from the mountains that surrounded Marseille.

Marseille is the oldest and southern-most city in France, and the second largest after Paris. An ancient Mediterranean port, Marseille dates back to the Roman Empire and started to flourish as a trading center when enterprising Phoenicians rowed there in the seventh century BCE. When we were there, the city was better known for its rough edge. Gangsters ruled the streets; caverns beneath the narrow medieval alleyways concealed gambling, murders, drug trafficking, and all sorts of other sordid activities.

Marseille was also infested with rodents. Huge rats poured out of the docks along the Mediterranean, and scurried along the streets and boulevards. A large fat-bellied rat invited itself into our hotel early one morning. I didn't know it was in our room until I felt something tugging at my shirt. I woke up startled, but didn't panic or scream. Leo, hearing me squirm, sleeping next to me on the floor, woke up and casually shooed it away. Now it was simply running wildly around the room, and Leo was instructing me to open the door so he could maneuver it out. Mama, of course, woke up when she heard the commotion, remaining calmly in bed until the rat disappeared. None of us panicked at the rat's intrusion. We were now conditioned to accept anything that was out of the ordinary. Nothing surprised us. Nothing surprised me, not anymore. My little body was drained of emotion.

Papa and Sam were already out in the street having coffee and smoking at one of the outdoor cafés, eavesdropping on every word they could hear from those sitting at the other tables and the passersby. Marseille was Papa's kind of town, where risky behavior was as deep rooted as the ancient buildings, and the bustling sounds of the city were sweet music to his ears. Mama was the one who did the worrying, fearing what would come next. Papa tried to assure us that we were safe now in Marseille.

"Max, we can't live like this for too long," Mama said to him later that day, her voice fatigued.

"I'll think of something, ask around for help, even if I have to give away the diamonds to get us out," Papa lied.

"Don't be afraid," I said to her in Yiddish, and in a trembling voice.

"Oh, Freddy, I'm not afraid," she said softly, but she didn't pursue probing Max on his thoughts about maneuvering us out of this terrible ordeal.

Each day, Papa and Sam would go out for an hour or so, looking for food, trying to pick up ideas on how to escape from France, asking strangers for advice. Though the refugees used their common difficulties to build friendships, they were careful not to disclose their plans for escaping, if, in fact, they had any. Revealing those secrets would attract a lot of people to follow the same course, and jeopardize everyone's chance. No one blamed anybody for this stinginess. It was understood that people had to devise their own schemes.

A few times Papa and Sam were stopped by plainclothes Gestapo. They were asked to show their ID cards to prove they had a place to stay.

Mostly, the Gestapo, along with the French police, sneaked into hotels and boardinghouses searching for the writers and artists Hitler sought. "We know what kind of refugees they're looking for," Papa told Mama. "We don't have to worry now."

"Max, you can't trust them to leave us alone," Mama cautioned. "You can't trust anyone. Be careful who you talk to when you go out of the hotel. Don't do anything stupid that will get you arrested," Mama warned him, looking to Sam and saying, "Watch your father."

Our hotel wasn't too far from the harbor, and a few times Papa went there to get passage out of France. Lots of refugees begged for boat tickets, but they did not come cheaply, sometimes costing as much as $500 per person. The diamonds would have covered the expenses, but he decided not to barter them for freedom. The people at the harbor he dealt with were mostly unsavory characters, and Papa was afraid that they would rob him if he said he could pay in diamonds.

The days and nights passed slowly. For me, there was nothing to do. I didn't yet know how to read, though Mama and Leo read for me some children's books donated by the Red Cross. But they didn't feel what the words said, sounding them out as if giving me a lesson on learning to read. I was bored. Mama wouldn't let me out of her sight, and neither would she allow Leo to take me somewhere alone. And Leo would turn twelve in September. He too must have rankled at our confinement.

Thanks to the concierge's wife bringing her yarn, Mama kept busy knitting sweaters for the family, thinking ahead of the coming fall season, and yet also worrying whether we would ever see the fall. She did spend time in the hotel's tiny lobby where she sat on the sofa and simply went on with her knitting. I spent the time doing much of nothing as I had no playmates my age. Leo did meet a few young Jewish boys and girls his age, and they mainly talked, sometimes laughing together, and listening to music on the radio.

Sam, as I said, was my father's companion, though not always. He hung around with a few teenagers who were also in flight, and occasionally their parents gave them permission to go together to a nearby café to eat and talk, talk mainly about their lives before the war, where they lived and went to school, what movies they had seen, books they had read, all the things that they were missing now.

One day when he was with Papa, Sam asked why he felt obligated to his younger sister Hedwig.

"The same reason you came back from Pau to get us out of Gurs," Papa replied. He looked lovingly at his oldest son, his eyes filled with tenderness and pride when he told him what he didn't have time to say when he returned to rescue us. "I gambled with your life. I know I shouldn't have done that. It would be better if we stayed together, even in death, I thought, when you were gone. But you came back to save us."

Father had called Hedwig to tell her he was now in Marseille. He and her family would follow within a few days, with Papa putting them up at a nearby hotel. From now on our journey would be their journey, with both families joined in a battle to survive Hitler's march across Europe.

After he had finished with the phone call, Papa and Sam took their customary walk, smoking cigarettes, often down to yellow-stained fingertips. Yes, Sam was following in his father's footsteps and vices. Surprisingly, Mother accepted Sam's new habit as a part of life. Again, nothing seemed out of the ordinary in our life on the run.

Then it happened—an anti-Jewish decree that unleashed the first sign of the Vichy government's collaboration with the Germans. On 27 August, the government abolished a law that banned the French press from spreading attacks "against a group of people who by their origin belong to a specific race or religion, when this attack is intended to stir up hatred among other citizens or inhabitants." Lifting the ban gave the press a free reign to spread hostility about the Jews. Vichy's proclamation uncorked strong feelings of anti-Semitism among the French, with newspaper articles accusing Jews for France's defeat to Germany and raising the specter of Jew baiting that were seen as consequences of its surrender.

Hundreds of thousands of fleeing Jews in southern France, 191,000 foreign Jews alone swarming into Marseille, all of us would have to get on the road again. But where would we all go?

The anti-Semitic weekly newspaper *Gringoire* published a regular column entitled "The Jewish Problem," which had circulated in Marseille. The first sentence of one column was enough to send chills through the huddled masses of homeless Jews—and exhume among numerous Gentiles their deep-seated hatred of Jews for killing Jesus Christ: "One has to be naïve to think it that it [the problem] has just come up. It has existed for two thousand years."

Vichy propaganda also blamed Jewish refugees for the shortage of essentials such as food, butter, and soap, and for the meager rations the French had to accept. The *Gringoire* fed that resentment: "How long shall we feed these undesirables, more accustomed to using a revolver and a bomb than a pick and a shovel, while our children, our women and our invalids lack milk, meat and bread?"

"What does this all mean?" Leo asked, his face tense with fear.

"Oy, es nicht git, Max," Mama declared: "It's not good."

"I don't know what it means for us," Papa admitted.

"What else will the newspapers write about us Jews? What are we going to do?" Mama wondered. "Let's not give up on going to Spain. Why can't we do that? It's our only hope, and all we're doing here is waiting for the Nazis to get us."

His face creased with fear, Papa's answer did not reassure her. "We need to get an exit visa to get out of France, a transit visa to cross into Spain, and an entry visa to get into Portugal. And Portugal won't let us in without passports, and how are we ever going to get a French visa now?"

I didn't understand what was going on, but my brothers did. Just looking at their expressions frightened me. I leaned against Leo for comfort during the discussion in the hotel room. I depended on my brother to guide me through this confusing and often terrifying crisis. Leo didn't talk much. His face, though, could speak volumes. A turn of the lip, a raise of the eyebrow said as much as the few words he uttered. Holding hands with him was enough to make me feel secure.

According to their identification cards, my parents did as much as they could to find a legal way to depart from France. Papa and Mama went to the Belgian consulate in Marseille on 3 September, a week after Vichy gave the press free reign. Papa knew that a visit to the consulate would be futile, but Mama insisted. My parents had lived in Belgium since 1924, but remained citizens of Poland, which meant that the Belgians could do nothing for them. "We need your help," Papa pleaded with officials. "Just change our nationality to Belgian, and we'll take it from there." He was going to bribe them with diamonds. "You know, they're everywhere here, and we have to be careful not to get into trouble," a bureaucrat said of the Gestapo. His voice seemed to anticipate a Nazi raid into his office. "I'm sorry we can't do anything for you."

Throughout September, Papa tried to get us out of France, lining up with thousands of others at various consulates, hoping to find the right person who would sympathize with our plight. The Portuguese got tougher with refugees, issuing visas only after approval from the government in Lisbon. And lacking an entry visa, a transit visa to travel through Spain was impossible to obtain.

Papa was worn out, his small, lean body turning frail, and his curly hair thinning. His teeth, stained with nicotine from years of smoking, were loosening from lack of healthy food. Five months of running, hiding, imprisonment, and food rationing had weakened him. Mama didn't look well either. She wasn't as gaunt as Papa, but she looked more tense than I had seen before. Nothing was rosy for her or about her anymore.

We had now been in Marseille for six weeks, since 18 July, cooped up in that little room in that noisy, crowded hotel in the center of town, weary of the French police hovering over us, restless from lack of sleep, my father snoring like he was sawing wood, my mother's face fallen, Sam and Leo angry that my parents refused them permission to wander alone around town.

When Papa went out, Sam always accompanied him. Papa feared going out at night, certain that he would be arrested for loitering, and simply vanish forever.

Occasionally the entire family ventured out, but only to go to a café, mostly for breakfast, to relax and have coffee, or eat croissants with cheese, but mostly to watch and listen for information. But that was Papa's job. I just went along for the ride, captive not only to the war, but to my dependence on my parents.

Then something happened, something far worse than lifting the press ban against attacking Jews. "They're going to do something that's not going to be good for the Jews," Papa explained to Mama, who could not read nor speak French well. "They're going to force the foreigners, men only, into work camps, from the ages of eighteen to fifty-five, and also define who is a Jew and who is not."

Mama was enraged. "They're doing to the Jews what the Nazis did in Germany. The French are damn Nazis. Max, we have to get out of here, quickly."

Germany's Nuremberg Law defined anyone with three or more Jewish grandparents as a Jew, regardless of whether that individual identified himself or herself as a Jew or belonged to the Jewish religious community.

On 3 October, the French government approved a set of racist laws known as Statut des Juifs, which were similar to the Nuremberg Laws. The Statut des Juifs excluded Jews from working in most professions, particularly those that influenced public opinion. Jews would be summarily ousted from positions in the press, radio, movies, and from French schools, colleges and universities (all of which had employed many eminent Jews), as well as from holding top public service positions and serving as officers of the armed forces. The new humiliating and inhumane laws of the French state were a hammer to break our spirits.

Another set of laws passed on 4 October dealt with foreign Jews and read: "The foreign nationals of Jewish race will be able upon passage of this law to be interned in special camps by decision of the prefect of the department of their residence." Sam's escape from Gurs and his return to free us now grew from bravery to superheroism. If we had remained in Gurs, the chances of our survival would have been nil.

"Some months later, Prefect Chiappe would never have signed the laissez-passer," observed Natanson, the French college professor and Holocaust historian, who had responded to my e-mail that Thanksgiving 2001.

Both laws were not published until 18 October, but Mama and Papa already knew enough to make their next move. On 8 October, the day I turned four years old, Papa and Sam went to the police. What Papa asked for, I don't know, and neither does Sam, though decades later I was fascinated by the reply, found recorded on Papa's ID card. It was stamped with the seal of the Police D'Etat, the national police, in Marseille. Written across it was the word "Recuse," meaning denied, and the date, "8/10/40." Who knows why Papa went to the police? The police didn't issue visas, but sometimes the prefect required applicants to obtain a certificate of good behavior from the police before a visa was issued. Did the police refuse Papa's certificate? I don't know. We know Mama didn't go with them because her ID made no reference to that visit. I want to believe that he didn't take with him the entire family out of fear that we might be arrested and returned to Gurs, or assigned into a forced residence, or worse fate. Luckily, he and Sam were not arrested.

Papa had also heard that an American was in town helping the most culturally well-respected German refugees of that time, many of them Jews, escape from France, some illegally over the treacherous Pyrénées to Spain, and aiding others by bullying and cajoling the American consulate into granting them visas to enter the United States.

The American was Varian Fry, who conducted an underground operation from a Marseille hotel and is credited with saving thousands of lives. Unfortunately, Fry did not have enough American support to assist every refugee that sought him out, and I can't say if Papa was among them, though I believe he had learned on the street about Fry's operation.

Papa tried to get a US visa on his own. He joined thousands waiting outside the consulate one day, staying in line for hours, braving the damp cold in his worn-out suit, skinny as a rail, his hands wedged deep inside his suit pockets to keep them warm. Again, officials were ordered to approve visas only for writers and artists hiding in France and for fleeing Jews who had rich relatives in America who could promise them well-paying jobs. Papa made repeated efforts to phone his wealthy New York relatives. He didn't get through. Papa tried again a few days later, phoning a particular relative at his Manhattan office, only to have the person on the receiving line tell him that the relative was not available, and Papa had also written letters, none of which were answered.

Papa realized it had become too dangerous to remain in the hotel, now that the police knew who he was. He was scared that they would set a trap and arrest not just him, but our entire family. He agonized about telling Mama what he had done, and was afraid he would be discovered if she looked at his ID. He woke her up in the dark of the night and ushered her out of the room to whisper to her what he tried to do.

"I'm afraid of the police now," he told her. "We are going to leave in the morning. We can't take any chances staying here a day longer."

"Why didn't you tell me that you were going to do this?" she asked. "Maybe if we went with you, they might have had some sympathy for all of us, especially the children."

"It was too dangerous," Papa said angrily.

"So, what are we going to do?" she mumbled in resignation.

That morning we left Marseille by train, but this time we were not empty-handed.

Sam: There was this guy who kept on going to Belgium and coming back to bring stuff for people. He was in the same hotel, and we asked him to stop in Paris-Plage, and he brought back to us the four valises.

Sam remembered him as a very nice man who simply wanted to help. The man risked his life, traveling 650 miles each way to retrieve our luggage from the warehouse at the small beach resort we escaped through to stay one step ahead of Hitler. For the moment Mama's strain on her face showed relief as she pulled from the cases clothing for us all, clean and fresh, and knowing her fondness for nice clothes, she had packed the best for us to wear. The past week Mama seemed to be withering. She probably couldn't wait to dress me in my clean clothes, perhaps rejuvenated by the idea of making her little Freddy look handsome. I can just see her dressing me in my favorite outfit, a tweed suit, short pants and matching jacket, clean socks and shoes, and showing me off to the hotel guests huddled in the lobby. "Oh, monsieur, tu es trés joli," Sir, you are so pretty. I could just hear the women cooing, to my mother's delight, the compliments restoring her spirits, restoring ours.

Chapter 15

Safety in the French Riviera

Mama: Then we went to Nice, and that was it, and when Hitler came, we had to go into hiding.

Her barebones statement again left a gaping hole for me to fill. Fortunately, my childhood memories and understanding were maturing, so I didn't have to rely totally on my mother and brothers' recollections. In some ways, it was a relief for us all. I could finally feel that I was coming into my own as a narrator; the events had happened to me too, me, as a real participating person. And my mother and brothers were spared some of the exhaustion and pain of remembering, of fleshing out my life for me.

We left Marseille by train soon after my fourth birthday and headed east toward Nice, a town under Italian jurisdiction following their invasion of the French Riviera, which had come to be known as the Italian Zone. I was bracing for the worst, anticipating danger at every turn. I imagined that we would be stopped at a checkpoint at the railroad station, where police would demand Mama and Papa present their identification cards, and mean-looking men would cast suspicious looks at us. Thankfully, I didn't see any of that. Instead, I ambled out into the street to be greeted by a sun that bathed us with warmth and seemed to bow its head in welcome.

I felt as if I was whipsawed, one moment feeling the unbearable strain of the ordeal of war and being a refugee, and the next moment walking out of its long shadow into the sunny and gentle wind of the Riviera.

There was a seamless parade of people dressed in light clothes, men in sleeveless shirts, women in breezy dresses, many of them white cotton. And the children wore colorful outfits, dazzling compared to my heavy shorts and scruffy shoes.

I got angry, jealous of their clothes. They were showing off, as were the buildings, dressed in their summer colors of whitewashed white, pink, light green. I felt oddly uncomfortable being near the beauty of these buildings, thinking I didn't belong there.

Mama, holding my hand, walked cautiously through the daylight, not knowing what to expect, nurturing that suspicion that would linger in her for the rest of her life. She probably had to pinch herself to believe that we were in this kind of place. She took a deep breath to fill her lungs with the clean, crisp air. But she was bothered by the thought of the demands it would place on Papa to take care of us amid this elegance and luxury.

"Max, I don't think we can stay here long," she said tenderly, though disappointed she had to say it. "It's going to cost us too much money."

"We're going to sell the diamonds to get cash," Papa said coldly, misreading Mama's feelings. "This is where we will stay."

Papa was in no mood to talk, as his thoughts were on finding somewhere to live. He sped up his pace to walk ahead of Mama, which seemed a sign he wanted to be left alone. He turned to the first shop he saw to buy a pack of cigarettes and a handful of cigars. Papa carefully unwrapped the plastic cover protecting one cigar, snipped the end and moistened it with his tongue, and lit up to savor his first puff since leaving Marseille.

Nice is the capital of the French Riviera, where the rugged Alps shelter it from the cold northern winds, and the ever-blue Mediterranean Sea brings in the warm, soft breeze that we were to enjoy for the next two years. Founded by the Greeks in the fifth century BCE, Nice has had a mixed relationship with Jews. The Statutes of Nice enacted in 1342 forced Jews to wear the dreaded yellow star, as they had to throughout Europe during the Middle Ages. So, Hitler was by no means the first ruler to force Jews to wear this humiliating, and shameful cloth label. On and off for centuries, depending who was the ruler at the time, the Jews of Nice were forced to live in assigned sections chained off from the rest of the community, similar to the relocation of Jews into ghettoes during Hitler's regime. Only for a brief period, following the French Revolution, were Jews granted their liberties. They were returned to the ghettoes in 1828 when a new administration took over. Finally, Nice granted Jews their civil rights in 1848.

We stayed for a few days in a sleazy hotel in the back alleys of the town. There, Papa heard from other refugees of better places to live. My parents chose a fancy hotel, the Hôtel Continental, as our residence. A few weeks after settling into our room, Papa phoned Hedwig in Marseille to tell her to come to Nice, and they came in December. The Katz family initially stayed at Hôtel L'Escurial, but that was too expensive, and soon they moved to another part of town where they rented a cheap apartment. We remained at our hotel until August 1942, that terrible period when foreign Jews living in Nice were rounded up for deportation to the Nazi death camps.

Hôtel Continental was a popular British tourist attraction described in a brochure that Mama kept until her death: "Ideally located amidst its wonderful garden, the Continental, with its luxurious yet restful atmosphere, is a home to those who seek the charms of the city with its delights of home-like, elegant living quarters."

Hôtel Continental was a fairytale mansion. It was my home and it was beautiful. Plenty of palm trees and flowers adorned the garden, whites and yellow blossoms surrounded by green, lush plants. They were perfectly arranged around manicured mounds, with a palm tree in the center of each mound. Benches along the curved walkways inside the garden provided comfortable shading from the sun. Mama loved sitting with other refugees residing there, including the Kurz family.

Built at the turn of the twentieth century, the Continental was a huge rectangular hotel, with rows of windows and sculptured ornamental decoration on its façade. A long gravel-paved driveway bisected the garden and allowed an amazing view of the small towers atop the hotel, of a magnificent cathedral-style dome to the left, and of the main entrance's marble stairway.

I remember standing at the top of the stairs shouting obscenities down at my best adult friend, an Italian military officer, for betraying me. But that was later, in August 1942 when the Nazis and the French police were fanning out all over Nice to round up thousands of Jews for deportation to Auschwitz.

Upon entering the hotel, one walked through a spacious and tapestry-rich hallway decorated with huge pots of leafy palms, sofas, and lounge chairs. Each time I passed through, I felt as though I was living in a *real* castle, not at all like the abandoned one we had hidden in a few months before. Greek-style pillars framed the archways and galleries that lead into the smoking salon where adults played cards, the private salon for meetings, and a large restaurant marked by elaborately ornate wood molding and crystal chandeliers.

I can still see the concierge behind the desk, a robust woman who spoke with a rough, low voice and dressed mostly in dark, somber evening gowns. Her black hair hung loosely over her ears, and gave her a mean look. I tried to avoid her as much as I could, usually taking the long way to exit.

Hôtel Continental housed the Italian consulate, which used the entire west wing for its operation. The Italians, though allies of the Nazis, were to play a crucial role in protecting and alerting us to the presence of the Gestapo and the French police. The Nazis and their collaborators regularly came unannounced to the hotel to try to catch Jews violating Vichy regulations such as failing to carry identification cards, breaking the rules on food rationing, or conducting black market business. My brothers made friends with two of the consuls, and the Italian officer assigned to guard the consulate became my pal.

Our three-bedroom apartment wasn't nearly as elegant as the public space. We lived on the top floor in a corner apartment with a large living room that faced the garden, a bedroom for my brothers, and a small bedroom for me. The living room had a large closet to store the clothes we would eventually purchase, and three windows that gave us a beautiful view of the garden. My parents' bed was in a corner of the living room.

My room faced the side of the building and had a window from where I saw the back of two-storied apartment houses. An iron fence, which went around the entire hotel, separated us from the French citizens living in these homes.

Mama dressed me in pretty summer clothes, and I remember one day being mistaken by a little girl from the other side of the fence for another girl. I think it was because of what I wore, a polka-dot shirt that was buttoned to matching shorts. The hat that I wore also matched the outfit and looked like a soup bowl. The little girl asked another boy that I had met, "Is that a girl?"

My friend did not like that remark, and told the girl what he thought. "How can you say that? Doesn't he look like a boy?" I was too stunned to say anything, and was grateful he stuck up for me. He was about my age and lived with his mother in a fancy suite on the floor below. He had a brown complexion that stood out when he wore light clothes. His mother was a very graceful woman who seemed to float on air when she walked, especially when she wore her noiseless straw shoes and flowing white dresses. She always covered her head with a white, silk shawl. The boy's name was Mickey Abet, though I'm not sure about the spelling of his last name. I was told that he and his mother were part of a royal family in Turkey and that his father had recently died, or was killed.

I think the name Mickey was a version of his Turkish name. He was a Muslim and became my first best friend. We played together and rode our bicycles around the garden. I spent many hours in his apartment, which was decorated in ivory colors from carpet to curtains.

Mickey and his mother had a live-in nanny. One day, Mickey handed me a popgun and dared me to aim it at the young woman. I hesitated, but he insisted. From about 15 feet away, I took dead aim and hit her on the left side of her cheek while she was sitting on the sofa knitting. The shot stunned her, and I regretted it immediately as the side of her face reddened. I think Mickey was more ashamed than I was, and watching her suffer, he rushed to give her a tender kiss on the cheek. We were, in fact, just boys, and we did the things little boys do, physical games, mischief. Even though our position in Nice—and in the world—was tenuous at best, we couldn't stop being boys.

I even had a girlfriend. Her name was Sonya, and she frequently hung out with Mickey and me. She lived in the hotel with her parents, also Belgian Jews. She had curly blond hair that hung over her shoulders, a perfectly round-shaped face without flaws, at least none to my eyes, and she wore beautiful dresses, mostly white with frills around her short sleeves. Even at my age then, I would stand in front of the mirror and carefully comb my hair before seeing her. She loved smelling the flowers in the garden. I don't remember anything about her other features. Of the many photos I have from Nice, none were of Sonya.

Then, one morning, I found that Mickey and his mother had left the hotel, without saying goodbye. I remember feeling so lonely and afraid when no one answered my knock at his door. I guess I was afraid of disappearing myself—with no chance to say goodbye, too. I have no clue what happened to Mickey. Once we parted I never saw or heard from my friend again. And I don't know what happened to Sonya, whether she survived, or was slaughtered by the Nazis.

In Nice, I often went to the sea with my brother Leo and our cousins and friends who lived at the hotel. The Mediterranean beach wasn't sandy like the beaches where I spent my vacations in Belgium. Nice's was a gray pebble beach, the rocks rounded and incapable of bruising bare feet. Because our parents had to budget their money carefully, we seldom rented lounge chairs. Mama and Papa couldn't even afford to buy me a bathing suit. Instead I wore briefs to swim as did many of the other boys.

I enjoyed going to the beach and strolling down one of the world's most famous seashore walkways, the Promenade des

Anglais. In the distance, I could see the Palais de la Méditerranée, then France's top earning casino, where Papa loved to go, and where he became friends with a Catholic gentleman of Italian descent. Papa had told me the man's name was Consalo.

Many Jews made a living as black marketers, operating in secrecy, illegally selling luxury goods that were purchased by people who didn't care how much money luxury items cost. Jews were forced into the black market because that was the only way they could earn a living. Papa sold jewelry on the black market. Selling jewelry was one of the most profitable ventures, and there were plenty of wealthy people living freely in Nice who wanted to maintain their extravagant lifestyles.

Usually Papa was gone for most of the day, only returning home for lunch. And since there was no curfew, he spent many evenings gambling at the casino. Mama was upset that he was away that much, but she acquiesced so long as we had a roof over our heads and were relatively safe. Sam did little with his time. He hung out mostly with girls. Leo went to a school to learn the hotel business, but not for long. Everything was tenuous, even in that beautiful place.

Chapter 16

THE ITALIANS PROTECT US
FROM THE FRENCH POLICE

We didn't know it then, but coinciding with our arrival in Nice in October 1940, the Nazis deported more than 15,000 Jews living in the Rhineland, the lush-green and vineyard-rich countryside of northwestern Germany across from the French border. People were crammed into railroad boxcars and shipped to French concentration camps, including Gurs, where about a thousand died in the first few months from starvation, dysentery, and typhoid. Gurs now held 13,500 men, women, and children, the vast majority of them foreign Jews.

Also at that time, the Vichy government dismissed Jewish officers and enlisted men from its armed forces. Among those dismissed was my Uncle Emil, Papa's twin brother, who lived in Limoges, the same town where Hermann and his family lived.

On the war front, British, Australian, and Greek soldiers were advancing against the Italians in Libya, forcing Hitler to come to their rescue. The Germans and British continued bombing one another, killing thousands of civilians on both sides. In November 1940, the Nazis in Poland rounded up Jews and pushed them into a ghetto in Warsaw where nearly 300,000 Polish Jews were already living. Others deported there, including 40,000 Belgian and German Jews, swelled the total to more than 400,000. A month later, the Warsaw Ghetto was sealed off from the rest of the world, its future unknown; its fate bleak. Other ghettoes were created throughout Poland, including in Mama's rural hometown, Pabianice, into which the remaining Jews were crowded.

Despite Mussolini's alliance with the Nazis, the Italians, who occupied and administered the region of France that included Nice, protected us from the Vichy government. The Italian government refused to apply Vichy's anti-Semitic measures on foreign Jews living within the zone it controlled. Concerned about the growing number of Jews migrating to the area, Vichy, in an effort to counter the Italians' resistance, authorized the French police in spring 1941 to arrest Jews in Nice, Marseille, and Cannes who were suspected of being black marketers. Reports of these captures came from our Italian friends at the consulate in the hotel, who assured Papa and others dealing in the black market that they would be alerted whenever the French police began their search. Once Papa hid for about a week in the hotel basement to avoid arrest. He became extremely cautious in his business dealings thereafter.

The arrests were intended to frighten the Jews, and, as Henry Chavin, secretary-general for the police in the Ministry of Interior, told Marshall Pétain's chief of staff, Henry de Moulin de Labarthète, "This is just an hors d'oeuvre, of course." Chavin even came to the French Riviera to arrest some Jews himself.

My cousin Doriane's father, Chaskel, sold food on the black market in Nice. Food remained scarce and could only be legally purchased with coupons the government distributed to each household. Still, in order to feed families, many turned to people like Chaskel. He rode to the countryside on his bike and bought food directly from farmers, often returning with eggs, butter, milk, bread, and vegetables, and occasionally chickens.

Doriane: One day we heard loud banging coming from the radiators. It came from the Italian consulate. We gathered our food and hung it on hooks outside the window. We had time to hide the food because the elevators were not working.

The crackdown on black marketing led to the arrest of more than 700 foreign Jews. They were either sent to internment camps or into heavily guarded residences in the country. The capture of these Jews was just the beginning of the more severe dragnet operations that were to follow. Fortunately, neither my father nor his cousin Chaskel were caught.

In spring and summer 1941, the French police frequently sauntered into the hotel observing every refugee's move, sometimes searching them for illegal goods, or checking their identification. They even frisked my brother Sam, who was only seventeen, and demanded his identification, a green-colored card issued by the Vichy police that Jews were required to carry with them at all times. The French were looking for any justification to send foreign Jews to the concentration camps that dotted Vichy France.

On 2 June 1941, Vichy restrictions tightened further. Jews now had to provide information about themselves, their spouses, children, and ancestors, as well as family and given names, place of birth, date of entry into France, nationality, level of education and address. Papa and Mama obeyed the law, as did thousands of others, for fear of arrest. They believed that by complying they would not be harmed.

Mama and Papa kept up a convincing façade, allowing us to believe we were leading a normal life. With their heads held high and their beliefs firmly rooted in their religion, Mama and Papa proceeded to give Leo the ultimate gift bestowed on a Jewish boy turning thirteen—the opportunity to perform his bar mitzvah. In early October 1941, shortly after Leo turned thirteen, Jewish men, women, and children crowded into the synagogue, wanting to witness this wondrous and ancient ceremony being performed during these horrific times. Mindful that an assembly of Jews was courting disaster, Papa arranged for a few Italian policemen to guard the synagogue.

I remember sitting with the women behind the partition that traditionally separates them from the men in the main sanctuary. In Orthodox Judaism, men and women do not sit together in services. I didn't want to cloud this joyous day for my brother, but I didn't have such a good time. I remember sitting on a grey cushion way in the back, I think it was not even inside the main sanctuary, straining through the partition to see Leo up front as he chanted in Hebrew the weekly portion of the Torah, the entire scroll taking one year to complete, from the "beginning" to when Moses dies. Contained in Deuteronomy, the last of the Five Books of Moses, Leo chanted the portion where Moses tells the stranded Israelites who were once slaves in Egypt to be "strong and of good courage" as they prepared to cross the Jordan River into the Promised Land.

Even though I didn't understand what Leo chanted, I wanted to be near him to feel the thrill of becoming a bar mitzvah as I counted the years on my fingers for the day I would be standing where my brother was that day. All I knew what it meant to be a bar mitzvah was that you are no longer a boy, but a man. I was almost five years old then, but I wanted to be a man. This was not a time to be a child.

As I write this, it feels like I'm watching a movie of myself as I recall that day. I'm standing in the back of the theater looking at my younger self fidgeting around, wanting to be close to my brother Leo. Mama is with me, telling me to sit still, her head sometimes jerking a quick glance at the main entrance to the synagogue. Her face is pensive even in joy. I may not have felt it then, but as this scene unfolds, I'm afraid of what can happen, what the next frame will bring. Will the French police crash through the door, arresting all the men, women, and children? Will our Italian protectors be strong enough to resist them? And I wonder now, among all the Jews gathered to honor Leo, who in the end survived and who was murdered? How many?

We returned to the hotel when services ended, celebrating Leo's bar mitzvah with a few families who also lived there and with Aunt Hedwig and her family. Father presented Leo with an expensive Patek Phillipe watch, my brother's sole gift, but it was enough to make me jealous.

Two months later, in December 1941, Mama would take me to a department store to see St. Nicholas. Mama had once explained to me that Jews did not celebrate Christmas and that Santa Claus did not exist. I don't think I'd ever seen his image before, but I felt I should stay away from that bearded man dressed in red. Mama insisted that I tell St. Nicholas what I wanted for Christmas. The French version of Santa was slim compared to the portly Santa of America, but still he beckoned me to his lap.

"Freddy, go and ask him for what you want for Christmas," Mama said, giving me a little push in his direction.

I held on tight to the velvet-covered handrail and climbed the red-carpeted stairway to his throne surrounded with wreaths and chrysanthemums. My knees trembled. The man asked me what I wanted, and I told him, shakingly, a train set. He gave me a piece of candy, wrapped in green and red, and told me that I would get my wish if I were good. I couldn't wait to get back to Mama, and in my hurry running down the steps I tripped, the candy slipping from my hand. I jumped up and ran toward the safety of her outstretched arms.

"Freddy," she whispered, "don't be afraid. He wasn't going to hurt you. Let's get the candy." My hand clasped hers as we returned to the foot of those carpeted steps that rose majestically to the man and his gilded throne.

I never understood why Mother wanted me to go visit with St. Nicholas. Was it that he just happened to be there while she was shopping for clothes? Did she attempt to show anyone who might be casting a quizzical eye at us that we were simply Christmas shopping? We walked around the beautiful store that was bedecked with spiraling ribbons stretching across the illuminated ceiling that seemed stories high to that little boy, silver bells dangling everywhere, and trees glittering with lights.

Mother wasn't there to enjoy the sights, but to buy presents for her family, sweaters mostly, not for Christmas but for Chanukah, the Jewish Festival of Lights, which would begin the night of 14 December. So, was sending me up, no, forcing me toward St. Nicholas a way to hide that we were Jews?

Chapter 17

SAM ESCAPES TO PORTUGAL

In spring 1942, Papa heard reports that the police planned to pluck young, able-bodied Jews from their families and ship them to slave labor camps in eastern Europe, mainly to Poland, where they would make armaments for the Nazis. Sam, it was decided, had to sneak out of France and head for Portugal.

Mama: He got a visa to Portugal. He went to Portugal, and when Hitler came for us later, we had to go into hiding.

To Mother they were indistinguishable—Hitler, Vichy, French police—because their mission was identical: stripping Jews of all human dignities, first by scapegoating them, then by controlling them with anti-Semitic laws, followed by arrest and imprisonment, and finally by mass murder.

Sam: We were protected by the Italians until Vichy started rounding up people in Nice.... I left in April of '42 and you left in September, October of '42.

Sam couldn't just cross into Spain and then go on to Portugal. He had to weave through a bureaucratic maze to make his departure appear legal. First, Sam took a train from Nice to nearby Cannes where he visited the Portuguese consulate to obtain an entry visa, which was only valid for thirty days. Then, from Cannes he traveled nearly 400 miles to Vichy, the capital of Marshal Pétain's collaborationist regime, not a place for a Jew to be seen, especially those sought-after young men as Sam.

Sam: Father gave me an envelope and told me to go to Vichy where I would be put in touch with someone who worked for the government. We met somewhere, and when I gave him the envelope, he gave me the exit visa. There was money in the envelope. It wasn't that easy. I waited two weeks to get the visa and spent the time outside Vichy at a ski resort.

The person arranging this perilous meeting between Sam and the Vichy official was a relative of my Grandpa Feivel's second wife. After Grandpa's first wife died, he married a woman who had once lived in Vichy. Their marriage only lasted a few months, but it was enough to save Sam.

Sam needed one more visa in this maddening effort to save his life. After Vichy, he went to Marseille to obtain a transit visa allowing him to travel through Spain to get to Portugal. Rather than continuing on his travels, Sam returned to Nice, costing crucial days out of the thirty-day limit on his Portuguese visa.

Sam: It took days to get each of the visas. You don't just walk into the consulate and walk out the next minute with a visa. You had to wait to get approved, sometimes days. I wasn't the only one trying to get visas.

Why did you return to Nice?

Sam: I was running out of money. I didn't think I would be spending a lot, but I had to pay for hotel rooms and restaurants and I had to pack clothes to take with me.

Weren't you afraid you could get arrested?

Sam: Sure I was, but I had to take that chance. If I did nothing, that would have been far worse.

He returned to Nice—with an expired Portuguese visa, and one last time to say good-bye to his family.

"You're strong, Sam," said Papa, his voice betraying doubt that Sam would make it, but acknowledging there were no more alternatives. "You showed it in Gurs."

Sam kissed his parents and brothers tenderly on the cheek, saying to his worried mother, "Don't worry."

"Sam, I'm afraid for you," she said, her words filled with fear.

Mama wondered whether she would ever see him again, the tears streamed down her face. "Watch out," was all she was able to muster. He left just hours after his return to Nice, dressed smartly in a suit.

Sam's pilgrimage was charged with danger: at every stop, the French police boarded the train requesting to look at every passenger's identification paper, or French visa. "Samuel David Gross," the document read. A recognizable Jewish name, but nothing happened on the way. Was it because he looked so elegant and arrogant in his suit? Because he showed the social graces of a young man comfortable with wealth and intellect? Perhaps it was his fluent French with no trace of an accent? His highbrow behavior served him well since nobody stopped him throughout the 800-mile journey to Spain. Yet, all could have been lost at Pau.

Sam: I took a train to Pau to get an extension on my visa from the Portuguese consul. When I asked for the extension, the consul told me, "We received a telegram not to extend your visa." "I don't understand," I recalled saying. And he said to me, "Somebody must have tipped off the police that you were escaping." But he was sympathetic, and he told me, "I'm letting you go." He extended my visa, and in a few days I was in Portugal. I never learned who demanded my arrest.

So you left in April 1942, got the visas; how come we didn't leave at the same time?

Sam: Because Father didn't want to. He had no intentions of leaving. There was no particular reason. I don't know. He just didn't leave. Some people left, some people didn't leave. Maybe he didn't want to leave behind his sister.

Sam's destination was neutral Lisbon, the capital of Portugal, where he would live for the remainder of the war. Soon after arriving, Sam phoned to tell us he was safe.

Sam lived in a one-room apartment at a youth hostel and worked for the Polish government in exile, preparing and shipping care packages to Poland. Years later, I would ask him if the packages ever made it to Polish Jews. "I don't know," he replied. "I don't remember them being returned."

By 1942, Polish Jews were confined to ghettoes or hiding from the Nazi occupiers. That summer, the Nazis began an eighteen-month campaign to liquidate all the ghettoes, deporting millions of Jews to the six killing camps, all in Poland— Auschwitz, Treblinka, Majdanek, Chelmno, Sobibor, and Belzec.

The care packages—mostly food and clothing—were filtered through an elaborate underground network that dared to smuggle them into the ghettoes and distribute them to Jews in hiding.

Sam is burdened by guilt, thinking about his three years in Lisbon, not knowing then of the Jewish plight in Poland, of the extermination camps. "I had a good time in Lisbon," he said sadly, apologetically years later. "What else can I say?"

Chapter 18

SITTING TIGHT IN NICE

Two documents in Mama's old hatbox revealed that my parents may have also been making plans to leave around the time Sam did. There was a birth certificate for my mother issued on 16 March 1942 sent from her hometown of Pabianice, Poland, which was under Nazi occupation. It bore the signature of a German official named Bach and was stamped with a seal bearing the dreaded Swastika. The birth certificate noted that Mama was Jewish.

Wrapped neatly in another small package found in the hatbox was Papa's birth certificate issued from Frankfurt, Germany, 31 March 1941. It was marked with the same seal and signed by an official named Klebs. Papa was labeled an Israelite through his parents. "Father: Sculptor Feivel Gross, Israelite. Mother: Gisela, born Kurz, Israelite, both residing in Frankfurt am Main."

I was dumbfounded that the Nazi officials bothered to reply to requests from Jews. Were they merely carrying out their assignments? Or did a surge of remorse overwhelm these two government workers to do a good deed?

What's also intriguing to me about the birth certificates was that Papa received his a year earlier, in March 1941, though we all felt secure living in Nice then. A year later, the situation was different. Mama would later recount our numerous attempts to flee to America in the spring of that year. But this time it wasn't the French, but Papa's relatives in New York who stopped us.

They refused to submit the necessary affidavit to the US Consul vouching that we were honest people and would cause no problems. I learned later that these relatives rejected our plea because of another cousin they had vouched for in late 1941. The cousin was given a job at one of their factories, but dissatisfied with his pay, he soon after tried to organize a workers' strike for better wages. Our New York cousins were simply afraid that we too would cause them trouble.

Papa's cousin, Chaskel Kurz, and his family took no chances with their lives and fled Nice in June 1942 to Istanbul, Turkey, where they had connections. Chaskel, a food merchant, begged Papa to join him.

"Max, you have to leave here now, do you hear me?" Chaskel implored. "The police are arresting Jews and handing us over to the Nazis."

"Not yet," Papa replied.

"Max, it is dangerous to stay here," Mama shouted. "We have to go."

"We'll go, but not now."

Hitler's Final Solution to the Jewish Question was set in motion, with the Vichy government fully supporting the madness. In fact, the French authorities went one step further than the Germans, offering the deportation of children of foreign Jews in the unoccupied zone. The Germans had demanded only that Jews 16 to 45 be rounded up for deportation, not wanting to load children with their parents in the first convoys. On 20 July, the Germans approved Vichy's offer to surrender the children. Authorization to round up Jewish children for transport to the death camps came from Adolf Eichman, the SS officer in charge of organizing the deportation of Jews throughout Europe.

Fred Gross

And me? When those orders came out I was still riding my bicycle around the lush grounds of Hôtel Continental. But not for long.

Chapter 19

THE ROUNDUP BEGINS

Early July 1942. Out of breath after rushing down five flights of stairs, Mama shouted from the top of the hotel's marble front steps, "Freddy, come inside. *Quickly!*" Her tone of voice was edged with fear. *"Now!"* she bellowed. I dropped my bicycle at the front entrance, and ran with her up to our apartment. The Italian consulate had alerted Mama that the SS would be entering Hôtel Continental any minute. By the time we were upstairs, a convoy of black limousines and motorcycles had entered through the gate and parked on the far side of the garden.

Mama and I peeked out the window and saw German soldiers in combat gear hopping off their bikes to open the doors of the shiny, fancy black cars. Their superiors stepped out, dressed in tight-fitting uniforms and high black boots. The men didn't look fearsome from a distance, but the closer they came to the hotel, the greater Mama's fear.

I was too young perhaps to feel the panic. I should have felt it. I was simply curious. Their confident gait and the sheer power of the officer's appearance impressed me. A fleeting, strange, thought crossed my mind: I wished someday to be just like them. Strong. Soldier. Conqueror. Mama yanked me away from the window and hid us in the closet, leaving the sliding door slightly ajar to let in a shaft of light. Horror was etched on her face.

"What is wrong?" I asked angrily as I loosened myself from her grip.

"You stay here and I will tell you when it's safe to come out of the closet," Mama whispered forcefully.

I wished Papa and Leo were with us, but my brother was at the beach, my father at the casino. I missed Papa's strength and Leo's steadiness. I have no idea how long we hid. It may have been hours before Mama cautiously opened the closet door and went to the window. The Nazis were now gone. Mama knew when she heard the radiators clanging.

I don't know who these Germans were, but they seemed to be very important men. One may have been Theodor Dannecker, a high-ranking SS officer in charge of relocating Jews from France to the Polish extermination camps. In July, Dannecker was in the southern region visiting the internment camps, and probably came to Nice, aware of the large population of foreign Jews, demanding the Italians cooperate with the French roundups. Nice and the surrounding Mediterranean region were prized targets since about 25,000 to 30,000 Jews were living there, some 15,000 of them foreigners.

Whoever came to the hotel that day, our fate was now in the hands of Dannecker, a twenty-nine-year-old officer, who wrote to his superiors on 6 July 1942: "All of the stateless Jews in the Occupied and Unoccupied Zone will be turned over to us for evacuation."

Mama and Papa took the Nazi presence as a warning sign that the Italian consulate was losing its ability to protect us, and that the Vichy government was getting ready for France's darkest hour. It was time to prepare to run...again.

After the SS visit, our daily routine changed. No bike rides outside the hotel, no beach, no casino. We remained in our apartment, only to take short walks in the hotel's garden. Like the majority of Jews around us, my parents knew nothing about the gas chambers and were only vaguely aware of the harsh conditions in the mysterious places where Jews were shipped. Had they known of these atrocities months earlier, we probably would have escaped with Chaskel Kurz and his family in June.

History tells us that the Final Solution finally reached the unoccupied zone, and was put in operation 5 August 1942, when the French government sent memos to regional prefects. These messages spelled out which Jews to arrest and which to exempt. Foreign Jews, like our family, topped the list for arrest. The list of exemptions was so long that many of them were dropped, or simply ignored, so the French could meet Germany's demand to deliver 10,000 Jews in August. The next day, 6 August, began the days of terror. About 1,000 Jews trapped in the Gurs concentration camp were the first victims in Vichy France to be deported, sealed into cattle cars and transported by rail to a suburban holding pen outside Paris and then to Auschwitz. Other internment camps followed suit, the trains rolling away from France and into the Nazi death camps. My family, all of us, could have easily been cargo on one of those trains.

On 18 August, the Vichy government instructed the regional prefects to begin the roundups on 26 August. "Please keep this date strictly secret," the memo asked.

On 23 August, the headquarters of the Nice police issued a set of one-line instructions to its officers, leading off with this order: "This operation must be kept secret to the end," then "verify the addresses," which meant that the census on which Papa had registered our names in July 1941 would be used to track down Jews, and "make lists by localities and neighborhoods." Headquarters ordered all police to participate and that the raids be done "simultaneously and as quickly as possible…" "Railway station for loading, freight train, straw, buckets for water, toilet buckets, two guards per railcar…" and the final command: "Don't neglect anything—think of everything ahead so that the operation will be done completely, as fast and humanely as possible."

Vichy's secretary-general of police Lefebvre sent another message to the prefects at 12:10 P.M. on 24 August insisting that the arrests must take place on 26 August: "It is up to you to fix the starting hour of this operation to the time that suits you best. I would suggest strongly, however, to start in the very early morning, preferably between 4 and 5 A.M."

When the order came over the wire at Nice's police headquarters, the chief and his supervisors met to confirm plans for the assault. They pored over the lists containing the names and addresses of Jews and double-checked each officer's assignment. Though the order was to be kept secret, everybody at headquarters, even those with menial desk jobs, knew.

One police officer, however, kept his own secret, risking execution if he was discovered. After reading the final memo, he decided he could no longer remain silent in the face of the horrifying events unfolding before him. The officer waited until he got home late afternoon on 25 August and phoned Julius Kurz, a distant cousin to our family. The policeman told him that a raid would take place the next morning. It was twilight; a gentle breeze was touching the plants, flowers, and palms. Mama and Papa sat on a bench, and I was circling them on my bike. Suddenly, Papa saw Julius hurrying towards us. He got up, as did Mama, both noting his quick pace.

"Max, the police will be raiding the hotel early in the morning," Julius warned. "You have to go immediately, and leave everything else here. There is no time to pack."

"How do you know they're coming?" Papa asked.

"Why do you even ask?" Mama interrupted.

"I received a call from a policeman, a friend of mine," Julius said, heaving with anxiety. "I have to go and make some calls."

"I'll let my sister know," Papa asked.

"I've already called," Julius replied.

Papa and Mama found Leo around the corner at the side entrance to the hotel's kitchen. I followed my parents up the hotel's marble stairs, but stopped at the top when I saw my friend, the Italian military officer. "The Italians may have given us away," I had heard Papa say to Mama soon after Julius left.

I didn't understand what Papa meant, and thoughts were clouding my mind with confusion as the officer approached. Was he coming to me to say hello, or take me away from this place that I thought was my home now?

"We have to leave because you hate us, you hate Jews," I blurted out.

He was shocked. My friend looked at me strangely, as if he hardly knew me anymore, and trotted down the stairs without a word.

I wasn't finished. "You bastard," I shouted in French.

He turned around, and the hurt on his face showed how I had betrayed our friendship. He had to understand that I was caught in a moment of terror, and that I allowed it to grow into hatred. I hope he understood. I wish I could attach the officer's name to my pleasant remembrances of him. He rode me around town on his motorcycle, allowed me to watch him work in his office and he always greeted me with a taught salute. I can still see his pained expression, and I can't stop agonizing over it. I watched him walk down the long path toward the gate. We never met again. To this day, I wish I had swallowed my own hateful words before they reached his ears. But, then, I was only five years old.

"We waited too long to get out, and it's your fault," Mama yelled the moment we returned to our room. "I told you months ago we needed to leave. Why didn't we leave with Sam? We had our birth certificates, proper identification; everything was in order for us to get the visas. Chaskel begged you to leave with him, and now we're stuck!"

"If you want to go, then do it, but once you leave the hotel, they'll grab you," Papa slammed back. "You need me now, you understand. You can't do it without me."

The stress had become unbearable, and it was only reasonable that my parents had finally cracked. Mama picked up on my waning spirits and sat beside me on the couch, clutching me, protecting me like a bear would its cub from the harsh, uncertain world outside.

Chapter 20

A CATHOLIC FAMILY HIDES US

The street-smart voyager who was my father reached for his wallet and out came a small, shriveled up piece of paper bearing the phone number of the one man who Papa thought could possibly save us. He was a French Catholic of Italian descent named Consalo who lived with his family in Nice. He and Papa had become friends by chance at the casino, where their mutual interests bonded them into some kind of brotherhood. Papa called Consalo immediately

"I need your help," Papa began. "We found out the police will be raiding the hotel tomorrow morning to arrest us. Can you hide us out for a little while?"

The silence on the other end turned Papa's face into a white mask, but he maintained his composure.

"I'll have to ask my wife," the man replied. "Hold on."

Mama sat on the edge of the couch, clutching her hands in prayer, Leo paced back and forth, and I stood by Papa, as he waited.

"You come over whenever you're ready," Consalo told Papa.

"Gott sei dank," Mama exclaimed in German. Thank God.

"I don't want to take the chance of calling a taxi," Papa said to his friend. Consalo agreed to pick us up within the hour.

Papa didn't even bother to hang up the phone. He just pressed down the handle for the dial tone, and called Hedwig, hoping he would catch her before she and her two sons went into hiding.

"Hedwig, did you hear from Julius? He came to the hotel to tell us…." Papa couldn't finish his sentence.

'I know, Max. He told me the police was coming to get us tomorrow. Did you make plans to get out of the hotel?"

"Ya, ya. My friend Consalo is picking us up later to take us to his house. I don't know how long we can stay there." He gave her Consalo's phone number. "You know, we have to leave France, and we need your help, Hedwig."

Hedwig told him that the UGIF (Union générale de Israélites de France [General Union of French Jews]) was forging passports for Hedwig's family and gave Papa the number and address of the forger. The UGIF was a Jewish social service agency that, under Vichy authority, was intended to control Jewish activities and communal affairs. But during this tense period, it made up fake passports for Jews trying to escape from France. Hedwig had done volunteer work for the UGIF in Nice.

"We're going into the woods tonight near the farm where the boys worked. Oy, Max, will I ever see Sam again? I don't even know where he is. The UGIF is trying to find out for me. Watch out for yourself." Her husband Sam had been arrested weeks before the 26 August roundups.

"You get out now," Papa insisted. " Good luck,"

"Max," she said, "don't worry about us. Kisses to Nacha and the boys."

The conversation was not tainted with sentimentality. His mind was calculating the best way for us to leave the hotel without suspicion.

When the Italian friend arrived at the hotel to pick us up, Papa and Mama left all our possessions behind, except for one: my bicycle. I insisted. I had left behind my train set when we fled Belgium. I couldn't part with the last treasure I owned. Papa argued that the police may already be at the hotel to check if anyone was sneaking out, and that the bike might raise suspicion.

"You carry your bike and ride around the garden," Mama interrupted. "Max, let him do it. They'll think we're just taking a walk." I rode slowly from the hotel to the gate, my family a few paces behind. In less than an hour after getting the word about next morning's raid, Papa's gambling partner whisked the four of us away, with my bike tied to the top of the car. I didn't even turn around for one last glimpse of the place I had called home for almost two years. Two months shy of my sixth birthday, I understood now what was happening and desperately wanted to get to Consalo's home.

When I woke up the next morning, the morning of the raid, the breezy air blowing through the open kitchen window of our hideaway was as crisp as a starched white shirt. Eating breakfast with Leo, my view was of a neatly manicured garden with huge green plants that blocked the outside world from me. It was a relaxing way to enjoy a glass of milk and scrambled eggs, and to meet the Consalo family, who also had a boy my age.

Papa and Mama hid in the basement, which had a small bedroom and a tiny window covered with a flimsy brown curtain that allowed some light inside. The curtain remained closed, and one day when I pulled it open to let more light in, Papa just as quickly drew it shut, lecturing me that we had to be careful that no one discovered us. He flashed a tender smile that left me with a lasting imprint of that moment.

Papa's face was drawn, making him appear skinnier than ever. He wore thick-rimmed glasses, which he used mainly to read, and appeared studious and remote. In the hideaway, Papa did little more than read the newspapers until he could recite the articles word-for-word. Mama didn't read French, so all she did was worry. When they conversed, it was in a quiet tone. I visited with them once. I never went to see Mama and Papa at night since the basement light was always off. They lay awake in the darkness, afraid to fall asleep, taking turns keeping watch.

Upstairs, Leo, three weeks away from his fourteenth birthday, and I blended in with our hosts as if we became part of their family. We went to the market together, ate with them, and obeyed their orders not to leave the house without them at our side. We slept in a spare room on the second floor. If anything happened to Mama and Papa, the agreement was that this Catholic family would keep us until the war ended, and then make plans for us to travel to America to live with relatives there.

It was under these horrifying conditions that I experienced what should have been joyous and momentous. Going to school for the first time was part of my parents' attempt to maintain some semblance of normalcy, and to get me out of the house in case something awful would happen. Mrs. Consalo enrolled me at a parochial school, filling out the necessary registration forms with as much as she knew about me, including writing in my real name. She had made sure it was safe to attend this school and that no one except the principal and my first-grade teacher would know I was Jewish.

I sat about three rows back from the teacher's desk, right in the middle of the pack, lost in the maze of students around me. They sat obediently as the teacher talked. It was the first day of school following the summer recess, a chilly September morning. The teacher's dress was gray and heavy as drab and dreary as the day. She was short with a young face and black hair that fell down evenly on her shoulders. Her cheeks had a touch of pink. I sat quietly, hearing her words, but not paying too much attention. If she had called on me to repeat what she said, I would have blushed. She never called on me that day, although she glanced at me numerous times. She was keeping watch over me.

My first day of school turned out to be my last for quite awhile. The Consalos felt it was too dangerous to expose me so openly to the neighborhood children attending the school. They worried that the students might find out that I lived with the Consalos.

Two weeks after we arrived, the Consalos asked that we leave. The family was afraid that an informant would alert the police that Jews were hiding in their home. If they were caught concealing Jews, the police probably would have arrested them, too.

Papa's friend, Mr. Consalo, however, told my parents they could hide in an apartment he owned in the city, and that Leo and I could stay with his family. Mama and Papa needed to make a hasty decision, not about needing to leave, but about what to do with their sons.

"How can we leave the children with strangers? I can't get myself to do that, ever," Mama told Papa. "I want to be with them. I won't abandon them, even if it means risking their lives."

Papa felt as strongly as Mama, and so we departed together to hide in the apartment on the third floor of a tenement house. We brought with us the clothes we wore, and our trust in our new neighbors. "The people in the apartment building were very nice to us," Leo remembered. "They brought food and clothing, and came every day to see how we were doing."

A lot of tenants were in the building, and Papa and Mama feared that anyone of them could betray us to the police. "We can't stay here," Papa told Mama sometime between Rosh Hashanah and Yom Kippur, around the third week in September. "It's time to get the passports."

"We should also get in touch with Emil and ask him to help us," Mama said.

Uncle Emil was called in Limoges to help coordinate our next move, despite the police prowling in their siren-screaming vans or silent unmarked cars, searching for Jews. Being a French Jew, my Uncle Emil was safe for now since only foreign Jews were the initial targets of the roundups.

The Vichy police had met the goal of deporting 10,000 Jews, 9,872 to be exact, by 5 September. The roundups, which were conducted in full view of the public, began to subside, but Papa and Mama did not know that. Who would go and get the passports? Mama was the easy choice since the police could force Papa to drop his pants to see if he was circumcised as they thought all Jewish men were. Papa would have disappeared forever.

Nacha looked as if she was going to work, wearing a fall gray dress that fell just below the knee, covered by an austere black raincoat, her look softened by a dab of rouge on her cheeks and lips, and her hair all in curls, cascading down the sides of her face, stopping inches above her shoulders. She looked approvingly into the mirror, perhaps taking a mental snapshot to remember how beautiful she looked in case she were never to see herself that way again. She strode out with a confidence I had never seen. I felt safe and knew that she would return, unharmed by the police.

Still looking in the mirror, she said matter of factly, "If I don't return, watch out for the children and for yourself." Then, she turned to Papa and allowed her feelings to overtake her, permitting herself to embrace him. They held each other tightly, neither one willing to loosen their grasp.

"You must go now," Papa said.

Mama did not cry and seemed to relish the challenge of risking her life for her children's sake, a destiny that may have been foretold when she suffered through her lonely years as an orphaned teenager. She would not be the mother she had had as a child.

She kissed her two children, but was not mushy or teary eyed, and walked out as if she was going to take one of those morning strolls with me in Antwerp.

The morning rush hour served her well as she blended in with others who were walking to the trolley stop to go to work. She boarded the crowded streetcar, quietly sitting in an aisle seat. She pretended to read a Nice newspaper and clutched her purse, which held the photographs so vital to the fake passports. While she was gone, she called only once and that to tell Papa that she was waiting for the forger to insert those photos into the fake French passports.

Strangely, I wasn't worried about her, not even worried that she was in danger of being captured. And neither did Leo look worried, remaining silent through most of the day as I did. Papa smoked his cigarettes and listened to the radio, turned down low so that he could hear any noise that might come from the hallway, a shut door, footsteps, Mama's return.

There was a knock on the door. Mama returned in the first hour of darkness that same day. "Max, give me a cigarette, quick." She walked in resolutely and sat down, not even acknowledging our presence.

"Do you have the passports?" Papa asked as he gave her a cigarette. Mama motioned to her purse, too absorbed in inhaling and breathing out a puff of smoke. He examined the passports carefully, tracing his left forefinger over every line.

"Freddy, Leo, come give me a kiss," Mama called out.

"Hedwig called from Marseille to tell us that Sam and Manfred were rescued from a train that was deporting Jewish people to Poland. She said the UGIF helped them. A Catholic priest has arranged for them to go to Grenoble and stay for a few days until it's safe to go to Switzerland." We knew Sam her husband was arrested, but not her son Manfred.

"Are we going to meet them in Grenoble?" Mama asked in a wearisome voice. "Ich kann nicht mehr gehen." I can't go on anymore.

But she did, understanding that our safety was like a puzzle and that there were a few more pieces needed to complete it, and that Hedwig was crucial for those last pieces to fit together.

"Tomorrow," Papa answered. "She told us where to stay in Grenoble, and the telephone number where she could be reached."

Mama pulled herself up from the armchair and went to the closet to start packing a single suitcase. One was enough for this journey.

Later that evening Uncle Emil came to the apartment to pick up my brother and me—and my bicycle—to spend the night with him in a small hotel near the Gare de Nice-Ville, one of Nice's main railroad stations.

In the morning, Mr. Consalo picked up my parents and drove them to the station where we waited for them in a tiny enclosed area. The station was packed with policemen, roaming around casually, seemingly bored by their assignment.

"Don't worry, they're not arresting anybody. A lot of people are taking the trains up north, and they just want to keep order. I'll take the children, but you stay in my sight, and when you board the train, you go in one car, and I'll go into another car with Freddy and Leo," Emil instructed my parents.

"Be careful with the children," Mama told Emil, hugging my brother and me so tightly I thought it was our last time together.

It was nasty that morning, the sky as gloomy as the moods of the refugees huddled in the small waiting area. I heard a disturbing sound: a man crying. I was sitting on the bench, holding my bike tightly, when I saw a solidly-built man pass by me, wearing a camel coat, a dark brown felt hat, and light-brown leather gloves. He was hunched over, sobbing uncontrollably, his face cupped in his hands. The image frightened and confused me. We were on our way to freedom, weren't we? The police were not arresting us. What was wrong? Did this man know something we didn't?

He may have gotten word that some trains heading north were stopped by the police, who ordered Jews to get off, but at that time, none of us even imagined such a horrific thing. When our train, a normal passenger locomotive, finally opened its doors, a bevy of policemen suddenly appeared to take their positions at each entrance. Before I had taken one step up, an officer grabbed my bike, sternly telling me I couldn't take it onboard. I stared at him. He laughed.

Mama and Papa boarded one train car, and Leo and I, escorted by Uncle Emil, entered another compartment. We seemed safe under our uncle's protection, but with their fake passports, our parents were flirting with death.

152

Chapter 21

UNCLE EMIL AIDS IN OUR ESCAPE

Sitting across from Leo and Uncle Emil in the train on our ride north, I saw green fields and farmers harvesting their crop pass in the window. Cows grazed peacefully. Even at six years old, this carefree scene illuminated for me the senselessness of our predicament. Leo and I were deeply worried. If anything happened to Mama and Papa, would we be safe with Emil? Our uncle still carried some respect among his countrymen because of his military service in the French army, even though Vichy discharged him because he was a Jew.

Mama: In Grenoble we were hidden in a house, where a sister took care of us. She was so nice to us.

Whose sister? The sister of a family that lived in the house?

Mama: She was a nun, a Catholic sister, and the house was a convent that hid us and other Jews. The nun arranged for us to meet a paid guide—a smuggler—who was supposed to take us to Switzerland. Hedwig and her family hid in an apartment in Grenoble where other Christians lived.

We caught up with Aunt Hedwig and her family in a café, "dining on delicious Jerusalem artichoke gratin," my cousin Theo recalled. It sounds like a gourmet dish, but it isn't. Related to the sunflower, the Jerusalem artichoke was one of the few foods that could be bought without a ration card because it was easy to grow a lot of them.

Over dinner, the Katz family told the story of the death-defying way they all came to be together. Decades later, Hedwig, Manfred and Theo recalled the events.

Manfred: We found out that the roundup of foreign Jews would begin the next morning, August 26. We left the night before—my brother, mother, and I—to hide in the forest. That morning, I went to work like I did every day on the farm. About noon, a policeman came to find me at my address in Nice. A neighbor told him where I worked. I was arrested and taken by train to Les Milles, [a large internment camp outside Marseilles] where I found, to my surprise, my father. There, all the people assigned for deportation were assembled in the courtyard. A convoy was prepared for 150 men for the last car, including the sick, who were taken by stretcher from the infirmary and loaded up. En route, our train was attached to a huge convoy from Camp Gurs. Eighteen hours later we arrived at the Lyon rail station, where we heard voices shouting out our names. We were taken off the train and returned to Les Milles the following day.

The train's final destination was Drancy, a deportation camp outside of Paris, where Jews were assembled for their final journey to Auschwitz.

Theo: While the train is rolling to Drancy, Julien Samuel, the regional head of the UGIF, who liked Hedwig very much, saw that Sam and Manfred were on a dossier listing the names of those being deported. He intervenes and asks the police director that they be returned to Les Milles in order to expect the arrival of Hedwig and me, thus having the family united before being sent to Poland. They are taken to jail for the rest of the night, and the next morning with a gendarme they are taken to the train running in the direction of Marseille. While they are coming back, Hedwig has found a woman who had good connections in the camp. Hedwig gives her all the jewels and gold she has, and this woman obtained a leave for both of them to allow them to "go to a dentist" in Marseille. Marseille was a very dangerous place for Jews, who were chased in the streets like animals. When they left Les Milles, my father and brother were hidden in a film distributor's office where they stayed for the first three nights, and then my mother and I met them at the UGIF office on Yom Kippur. I remember that my father was covered with bug bites.

Aunt Hedwig: My husband and I spent so much of our free time in charitable activities in Nice that we were known throughout the city by Jews and non-Jews. But our good works had paid off. When the UGIF heard that my husband was being sent away they protested so strongly to the authorities that he was taken off the train and returned to me. It was like a miracle.

Uncle Emil made a practice run from Grenoble to small mountain villages near the Swiss border along Lake Geneva, particularly Annecy, Annamasse, and Monnetier-Mornex, all only a sliver beyond Nazi-occupied France. He practiced riding the train we would take, heading northeast, to determine which village provided the safest refuge. He reported back to Papa that Monnetier-Mornex, a tiny picturesque village nestled in the Northern Alps and 4 miles from the Swiss border, was the likeliest crossing. Hedwig's family went first, arriving by train at Monnetier-Mornex later than scheduled, at noon, when the police were not there to check each person's paper. They were out to lunch. The Katz family crossed into Switzerland 30 September.

The Gross family boarded the train in Grenoble two days later, eight days before my sixth birthday, Mama and Papa in one train compartment, and Uncle Emil, Leo, and I in another. As the train, packed with fleeing Jews, jerked itself forward, it took on a life of its own, controlling our destiny, deciding whether to dispose of us at each stop as the doors opened for the anxiously waiting predators: the Gestapo and French police.

Leo: The train stopped at each small village where the exit was controlled by gendarmes who checked the papers.

"Don't get off at the next stop," a kind-faced conductor whispered to my uncle, as Leo remembered it. "The police are arresting Jews there getting off the train."

Did he offer that warning to others?

Leo: I don't think he did. I'm sure he didn't. Imagine if he told everyone on the train. They would have believed the police was everywhere. People would have panicked. The train was moving, you couldn't escape, unless you wanted to jump out the window.

Uncle Emil was on edge, his face tense with fear, fists clenched, like a boxer ready to spring from his seat.

The afternoon sun glistened off the rocky French Alps dotted with snow along the top and greenery below. Small homes with gardens and patches of farmland along the railroad tracks greeted the passing trains. Children were lazily swinging on their swing sets, others were kicking a ball around in their yards. They were home from school, watching the train pass by them for the millionth time, just watching and waving to the passengers. Half-heartedly, I waved back. With the speed of a camera's shutter, all this exposure to ordinary life vanished as the train rolled into Monnetier-Mornex. Only a few passengers were left.

Uncle Emil got up from his seat and took down his leather suitcase covered with cracked lines from much use and age. We descended the stairs and dared to feel safe as the sun shone on the gray concrete platform. Ahead of us was the station's wrought-iron exit gate. As Emil, Leo, and I approached the gate, two French policemen suddenly strode forward from their guardhouse, which was hidden by bushes.

They wore blue, tightly fitted uniforms, with black leather straps winding diagonally around their bodies, and wide belts. The tough-looking officers stopped us as at the gate and ordered Emil to identify himself. He whipped out his French Army ID card, as my brother and I watched. They didn't ask us any questions, but if they did we would have passed muster because my brother and I spoke fluent French. After a moment, the gendarmes waved us on.

About 10 yards behind us, my parents were talking softly to each other, as Father cautioned Mother, "Say nothing when they ask you something. I'll do the talking." Mama spoke little French, unlike Father.

We slowly walked away, turning our heads ever so slightly to check on my parents. I saw Papa answering questions as the police carefully looked over their fake passports. The seconds ticked by. Papa answered a few more questions and the guards let them through.

"What is the purpose of your visit?" the policeman asked Mama. With her fake paper and accent, they would be lost. But, Papa intervened quickly to tell the officer they were just tourists. Mother filled this chilling moment with more detailed remembrances. As her memory came to the foreground, her voice grew louder, her face tightening with anger, and her lips pursing with hatred.

Mama: Uncle Emil was there before to check it out, and no police was there. When we came, there stood two policemen.

At the train station?

Mama: No, not at the train station. In the village, after getting off the train, there is a door, like a garden.

A gate, you mean.

Mama: Yes, a gate. So, Uncle Emil went through the gate and the police looked at Uncle Emil's papers, and they saw that he was French. They asked him, 'What are you doing here?' He said, "These are my children. I am taking a vacation here with them." So, they let you go. We didn't know where the hotel was, but Uncle Emil did.

Then we came to the gate, and they looked at our passports, and they let us go. And then all of a sudden we saw that they were running to you and Uncle Emil. Something wasn't kosher. When they ran up the hill toward Emil, we ran into this restaurant, me and Papa, and we had a beer. The people inside knew what was going on, and they were very nice to us.

Then, we saw through the window that the police were going back to the railroad station. When we saw that they went back, we left the pub. We paid for the beer, and went to Emil. We followed Emil to the hotel, and when we met him, he said to us. "You know, you were lucky. They were looking for you because of the passport." My passport had a French last name, but the name Gross was there as my maiden name. Since they saw that Uncle Emil was a Gross, too, the police asked Emil, "Are you relatives of these people?" He said, "I don't know them." And that's the story.

Those were the French police?

Mama: Yes, the French police, they were ruthless.

Emil, Leo, and I walked toward the hotel at the far end of the small Alpine village, the long, inclining narrow dirt road crunching under our feet deserted except for the three of us and my parents, who trailed at a safe distance behind. The road was framed on either side by patches of private homes wedged in between a mountain, which I later learned was Mount Saleve, which sloped down to the left of the village, leveled off to fit the residential part of the town into that space. The other side of the mountain, referred to as Petit (Little) Saleve, gently tilted upward to continue its path. It looked as if we were walking on a giant ladle. A few townsfolk stared and mumbled words of encouragement, knowing we were fleeing from the French police. Their village was a popular escape route.

"Be careful," some said. "Watch out, little fellow." But mostly, "Good Luck."

We had not eaten anything the whole day, our appetites choked by fright. But our hunger erupted as the hotel, located at the base of the mountain, came into view. We passed through its heavily decorated gates straight into the restaurant. There was no need to check in. It was here we would rendezvous with our smuggler, to whom we would entrust our lives for the price of $500. The waiter seated us in a section separate from the main dining hall. We were near the kitchen, but facing the front door. The five of us treated ourselves to a delicious dinner and accepted an offer from the maître d' of a free bottle of wine.

My childish curiosity drew me to tanks filled with live fish, shrimp, and lobsters. I walked over to the lobster tank, watching eerie creatures bunch together as if to keep warm, their bellies glued against the glass, eyes bulging, tentacles flailing, and their claws bound with rubber bands. I brought my face close to the glass, looked them straight in the eye, searching for some kind of sign that they weren't in any pain, some sign that they struggled to free themselves of each other so they could swim again. I saw nothing except that one creature broke away from the gang and lazily floated around. The waiter gently tapped me on the shoulder to tell me it was time to go.

"We are going to see each other again," Uncle Emil assured us. "Tout à l'heure." See you later.

"Tout à l'heure," repeated Papa.

Twin brothers united by birth, Max and Emil had a special bond forged initially by their differences, Max, the risk taker; Emil, serious and quiet. They learned from each other how to balance their lives, Max learning from Emil that life is a serious undertaking, and Emil learning from Max not to take life too seriously. Here fate had brought them together in ways that are unimaginable. Emil, the once physically weaker twin brother turned French soldier, risking his life to deliver Max and his family to safety. And hopeful they would meet again. Tout à l'heure. Uncle Emil planted a soft kiss on each of our cheeks and left to return home.

Chapter 22

WITNESS AT THE SWISS BORDER

It was dark when the smuggler came into the restaurant and took us through the kitchen and out the back door to a small shed with beds of straw covering the floor. We shared it with about ten other Jews, including a pregnant woman.

"You will have to be awake and alert for the crossing," the smuggler said, advising us to take a nap for a few hours. "I will wake you in the middle of the night."

When he woke all of us up, the smuggler guided us around the base of Petit Saleve, away from the areas with steep drops, and directed us through meadows and thick patches of forest, intentionally avoiding exposed hiking paths.

I was scared, really scared, more so than at any time in my long journey to escape Hitler. I even ignored the cold of that night. We walked. We ran. We laid down on the frozen ground. We hid in forests. We saw lights bouncing among a stretch of trees like ballerinas leaping effortlessly through the air, and then we heard the roar of engines.

We had climbed across the mountain to another village, Etrembieres, and reached the most dangerous part of our journey, the flatlands, the exposed farm fields where the trees were sparse and the search lights were crisscrossing so furiously fast that they seemed to be in panic, fearing they would miss their targets.

"Get down, and stay silent," the smuggler insisted. I learned later that the roar of engines came from trucks carrying French police. They patrolled near the border. They turned on floodlights to sight Jews before they could cross the French-Swiss border. After a few minutes, we resumed our flight, first crawling, and then running.

Mama: We were running to the border, and when we came close, the smuggler said, "You go now by yourselves. Walk fast, there is Switzerland."

Switzerland's Independent Commission of Experts in 2001, which issued a lengthy report on that country's involvement in the Holocaust, said of the smugglers:

> To actually get across the border, refugees often had to rely on a person who was familiar with local condi-tions—a so-called passeur—and then had to entrust their lives to him or her for better or for worse. Their distress was no guarantee of safety for the refugees; it did not protect them from theft or blackmail, or from being abandoned or even denounced by the smuggler after payment had passed hands. And even once they had crossed the border, the refugees were not out of danger since the Swiss authorities had established a seven-mile wide border zone in which refugees who were caught had to reckon on being turned away.

We still had to walk 2 miles to reach the border. Some in the group doubted our passeur. They were afraid that he would betray us to the French police scouring the area. A few went to the right, others to the left. Papa opted to continue straight ahead where the smuggler had indicated, and convinced a handful to follow.

Mama: And then we saw soldiers, and we thought they were Germans.

A soldier pointed a flashlight toward us, its powerful glow magnifying the shadowy figure into an unforgiving force. "Halt," he screamed in German.

We stopped, frozen in agonizing terror. "We are doomed," Leo recalled Papa saying, certain that the soldier was a Nazi. The pregnant woman beside me drew up all the fears stored inside of her, opened her mouth wide, folded her hands onto her belly, and released a terrifying scream. Her body went limp and collapsed to the ground, her fall softened by the grassy field. The soldier did not approach us to help her up. He was one step away from crossing into France. He stood his ground as we approached the Swiss border, where his feet were planted, and identified himself as a Swiss border guard.

Mama: So we went, and they stopped and held us. The Swiss didn't let everybody in, the criminals. They said if you have a relative living in Switzerland, you can stay. My mother was there, you see. I told the soldier my mother lived in Zürich and the police made calls to see whether my mother really did live there.

The Swiss soldier marched us to a tiny command post set back from the border. Leo and I sat on a wooden bench, watching our parents standing near the guard as he called the Zürich police for an answer that could save our lives.

Mama: We were lucky.

What did they do with the other people?

Mama: Sent them back.

They wouldn't even let them cross the border?

Mama: No, just think about it. Those mean bastards. It was scary, very scary.

Leo: That's why that young woman screamed. They wouldn't let her in. We were lucky.

The pregnant woman and the other refugees were dragged back to the French border, the Swiss guards using the butt of their rifles. Over the French border, the handful of Jews in our group scurried through the fields, their arms flailing in panic, their voices crying out for help. "Let us in! Let us in!"

Mama: They went that way; they went this way. They were captured. Oh, it was terrible.

Chapter 23

SWITZERLAND IS ALSO A PRISON

On 13 August 1942, less than two months before we crossed the Swiss border, the government of Switzerland passed a law sealing off its borders to fleeing Jews, just as the Holocaust reached high gear. Those who hoped to cross into freedom would instead be sent back to Vichy France, certain to be captured by the Gestapo or French police, and then murdered in the gas chambers.

Swiss historian Guido Koller described this law's passage as one of the most shameful episodes in Swiss history, "The law was passed just as the country's officials received reports of millions of Jews already slaughtered, mostly in Poland and Russia." Koller wrote that this information on the Holocaust came through in summer and autumn 1942. In Koller's *Hitler's Secret Bankers*, Koller writes, "The people in authority knew about the deportations, they knew that French and German policemen took Jews hostage, and they knew the deportations ended in the camps, where the situation was terrible."

Swiss churches and humanitarian groups condemned the law, pushing the issue so hard that the government backed down—somewhat. On 23 August, telephone calls were made to instruct border guards to accept Jews under sixteen, anyone with connections in Switzerland, families with children, old people, and pregnant women.

Still, Jews depended on the discretion of those guards. If guards felt the same way about Jews as the Nazis, they denied them entry. Others only allowed those with connections through. It seems that only that grandmother lived in Zürich saved us.

Unbeknownst to us, the smuggler had directed us to the most dangerous crossing area of the Swiss border. Switzerland's independent commission condemned in its report the actions of border guards in that area of Geneva in fall 1942.

> Many private persons and organizations, abroad as well as in Switzerland, helped refugees to cross the border and make it to the interior of the country. There were border officials who suffered a conflict of conscience and ignored regulations. Thus Switzerland admitted around 51,000 civilian refugees during the war, about 20,000 of which were Jews. The rejections and deportations in the canton of Geneva in the fall of 1942, however, make it clear that the contrary could also be the case. Here, refugees were deported by force and in part directly handed over to their persecutors. It has to be noted that the responsible persons were later tried and convicted for their unlawful proceeding.

When the Swiss confirmed that my grandmother resided in Zürich, we couldn't wait to reach her. At last, we thought, we were free. Instead, the border guards loaded us onto an army truck and transported us to a series of displaced persons camps run by the military. The first stop was Büren, 50 miles north of Bern, the Swiss capital, where Papa was delivered. The soldiers drove Mama, Leo, and me farther east to an isolated rural area in Münchwilen, a displaced persons camp 60 miles north of

Zürich. We arrived on the morning of 4 October. Conditions in Münchwilen were only a bit better than Gurs, though the soldiers and barbed wire reminded us of that earlier nightmare. The wooden barracks where we slept were sturdier and the food tasted better, though meals consisted of little more than soup and cabbage, anyway, at least the food was warm.

There were eleven children in the camp, mostly teenagers. I was the youngest, and slept with my mother. Our barrack had two-tier bunk beds that stretched from one end of the quarters to the other, straw for mattresses, and army blankets. The barrack had no heat, and we half-froze, especially during the winter. Many refugees caught colds, and frequently their throaty coughs kept us awake all night. Medical attention was scarce. I went to the bathroom nightly, climbing down the ladder with Mama, and trudging out to a basin to pee, in full view of the sentry.

The confinement irritated the women, and because there was no one to complain to, they argued a lot with each other. Mama was not above joining the fracas. I remember her telling off the woman sleeping next to us to stop taking our space. The army guards were on patrol around the clock, rifles on their shoulders. During the day, Mama and the others cleaned their families' clothes and were ordered to wash soldiers' uniforms. The children had little to do, except run around outside and throw snowballs. I was jealous of the older ones because they didn't have to sleep with their mothers. They had their own quarters inside the barrack.

One day, during a blizzard, I heard a commotion coming from the older kid's quarters, and raced to see what was going on, as did the guards. Leo and his roommates were engaged in a huge and escalating pillow fight. Leo was jumping wildly on his bed, swinging a pillow onto someone's head until the feathers flew out. The guards broke the game up and punished the boys by denying them food for the rest of the day. Even in such harsh conditions, young teenage boys couldn't help but be boys.

Papa's confinement in Büren, where he ran into Sam Katz and his two sons, was far harsher. The Swiss commission reported, "In many cases, living conditions in the reception camps did not even meet the simplest of standards: often there was no heating, the sanitary facilities were inadequate, and the diet was poor. Conditions in the camp at Büren which had originally been built for Polish military refugees and was converted into a reception camp in late autumn 1942, were particularly alarming."

Leo: Father told me the commander was a Nazi. He made them do backbreaking work day and night, sent them out with shovels to dig ditches along the roads, and forced them to chop down trees and haul them away.

Five weeks after escaping to Switzerland, the Germans invaded the part of France controlled by the Vichy government on 11 November. Hitler wrote Marshal Pétain that the purpose of the invasion was "to protect France." The real purpose was to deport more Jews. The Nazis soon unleashed a reign of terror against the 20,000 Jews still hiding in the Nice region. "Right until the last minute [before 11 November], the retreating Italians had done everything possible to save Jews," wrote French historian Paul Webster in his book, *Pétain's Crime: The Complete Story of French Collaboration in the Holocaust.* "The Consul worked twenty-four hours a day to produce hundreds of visas for entry into Italy and requisitioned trucks to ferry Jews across the frontier."

The consulate, headquartered at Hôtel Continental in Nice, where we lived before escaping the roundups, was one of the first buildings seized by the SS unit in the hope of finding files containing names and addresses of foreign Jews living in Nice, but these had already been sent to Rome. Livid with rage, SS officer Alois Brünner arrested and deported both the consul and vice-consul. They were the men who signaled us to stay in our rooms whenever the Gestapo or French police paid them a visit.

Chapter 24

MY SWISS FAMILY

In February 1943, with Papa still in Büren, Mama was given the choice of parting with her children so that they could be placed into private homes, or stay together at the displaced persons camp. Mama decided Leo and I should move to a normal household. Little did she know that the brothers would be split up. Our situation was not uncommon according to the commission's report:

> The separation of parents and their children— which raised legal problems too—was not due solely to regulations laid down by the authorities, but was also encouraged by the Swiss Committee for Aid to Children of Émigrés (SHEK). In the SHEK's opinion for the sake of the development of the children, a "normal" family atmosphere was preferable to living with their mothers in refugee homes.... SHEK managed to find foster families among the small Jewish community in Switzerland for only a minority of them. Most of the children lived in Christian families, which understandably led many parents to worry that their children would be estranged from their family traditions and their religious beliefs.

A Jewish family in Zürich took Leo. They owned a haberdashery in the shopping district and lived upstairs from it.

Observant Jews, the Lehrers celebrated the Sabbath in their home and attended synagogue. Leo was near Grandmother Rachel's home, and occasionally visited her and her ailing husband, the same man for whom she left her daughter behind all those years before.

I was placed with a Jewish family living in St. Gallen, but they were not observant Jews. A person from a Jewish relief agency chaperoned me on the train to St. Gallen, on the edge of the German border. We arrived in the snowy afternoon, and the chilly air seeped through my worn-out overcoat as if it were a sieve. The mother and father and their nine-year-old son David greeted me at the station. The parents were tall, thin, and had angular faces with almost razor sharp chins. The boy was the image of his parents and towered over me. They seemed happy to see me, though I thought the mother tried too hard to show her joy. The father was more natural and honest in his welcome. The son was another matter altogether. I sensed trouble immediately when our eyes met. Maybe it was David's height, so tall for his age, or his piercing silence. Something about him frightened me. I stiffened in his presence.

My new home stood on the outskirts of town among a row of two-story apartment buildings that seemed to run together forever, nothing fancy but better than any camp. I shared a small bedroom with David, our beds separated by about five feet of walking space. He stared at me curiously that first night, sitting on his side of the bed, following my every move as I settled in, never uttering a word.

The next day my foster parents were anxious to introduce me to their best friends, among them a woman in her thirties and her daughter, about my age. The woman was eager to talk to me alone and in French. She gave the excuse to my foster parents that her daughter was interested in hearing about my experiences. The three of us moved to another table. After I chatted a little bit about myself, the conversation turned to David. I don't remember the exact words, but the woman told me that David had problems and that I needed to be careful. The little girl said that sometimes he did crazy things, like go wild when he lost his temper, and that I shouldn't provoke him. "Please stay away from him," the girl pleaded. "I don't want you to get hurt." I took her words to heart.

Otherwise, I liked where I now lived. There was a small garden outside of the living room window in front of the house, and a huge farm in the back, separated from us by a low-voltage electric fence. It would sting when I touched it. The mother fed me well, and her hash browns, crispy on the edge, were delicious. I remember having long conversations with the father, Martin, mainly about nature. He taught me to identify plants and flowers, and took me hiking in the mountains surrounding the town of Appenzell, where we picked berries and sat quietly to soak up the panoramic view of the flawless rise and fall of sloping hills.

One day he suggested that I grow a sunflower in a small garden abutting the house. It grew to about ten feet high, and seemed to reach the sky from my view from across the street. I swelled with pride, knowing, but not yet fully comprehending until this moment in my writing, that I had accomplished something very important.

My temporary parents enrolled me in kindergarten. The school was about a mile away and tucked into a small valley where the trees far outnumbered the people. The kindergarten room had a long picture window that faced the woods. In the winter, I cross-country skied to school, and in the spring and fall I rode my scooter. When it was hot I walked in my bare feet.

I made lots of friends and met a teacher who became my guardian angel. She was young with an ashen face, her dark brown hair pulled tightly into pigtails that hung halfway down her back. I remember long flowing black dresses that reached her ankles and her black, laced-up shoes. She spoke to me in a soothing voice and watched over me more than she did the other children.

I started school in midyear and did a lot of drawing. She'd sit with me and ask about my drawings. On the first day, I sketched a picture of a house with a chimney that billowed black smoke and spread over much of the sky. A few birds were scattered about. She asked me to describe it, but I didn't know what to say, except to report to her what I saw. Here's the house, with a chimney, some clouds and birds flying. That's all I saw.

"What are all these black clouds?" she asked, her arm around my shoulder. "Were there bad people who did that?"

"Well, it's coming out of the chimney."

"What else? Can you tell me some more?" She gently pressed me for more information, and yet, what could I tell her? The features in the drawing said what I could not put words to, what I felt, and for a six-year-old boy that was enough. I didn't have the linguistic skills to express what had gone on inside of me when the German planes harassed us in the first few hours of my family's journey. My teacher knew that and she chose for me to draw something that could express my feelings, however the picture turned out.

Even then, after my family's long flight to safety, after all I had seen, I didn't yet grasp that planes couldn't fly and shoot by themselves. There were pilots and bombardiers in them, human beings choosing to terrorize and kill other human beings. As my journey had continued, those men inside the planes morphed into the guards and police and Jew-baiting citizens who also wanted to harm me. I was formed by that experience fleeing Belgium, as much as I was formed as a baby growing inside my mother. I had grown in those years we ran, in that world that wanted me dead.

I became possessed by the fear of harm—I feared it most during my teenage years, building an imaginary shield around me to keep others at a distance. I still see her, the one with the lovely face, resembling a teenage Elizabeth Taylor, her jet-black hair resting on her shoulders, following me in high school, in the hallway, behind me in the cafeteria line, even meeting me by chance on the subway one afternoon, and she telling me so gently that she wanted to go out with me, but it came over me, my heart pumping with fear, dismissing her rudely, my shield firmly in place. I turned into a lonely, silent youth and shunned many opportunities to have a social life with friends, to have a normal life. Saturday nights I would tell my mother that I was going out on a date, but instead would go out alone, sometimes riding the subway all night until it was time to go home. Other times, I went out drinking. I loved going to Birdland in Manhattan, listening to the giants of jazz—Dizzie Gillespie, Count Basie, Joe Williams—moving cautiously inside myself to the rhythm of the beat.

Many years later came the nightmares of crashing planes. In one dream, I sit in a lifeboat as a passenger liner crashes into the sea, missing me by inches. In another, a light aircraft would somersault down to earth while I was taking a peaceful walk on a country road. There were still others, and in all of them I was a little boy, and each time I woke myself up screaming. Would the fear I had learned as a child ever be unlearned? Would I always see the world as a place that didn't want me in it?

Even a year ago, April 2008, my wife and I were dining outside on a restaurant's patio, surrounded by spreading plants and flowerpots, and soft spring breezes. Yet, the roar of a passing freight train sent me diving under our table, images of a crashing plane flooding me with terror. The other diners, of course, remained oblivious. As I regained my composure and resumed my seat, I realized my dinner was now something to endure, something simply to get through.

I know I cheated myself by imagining harm coming to me. A confidant keeps reminding me, "The Nazis are gone. You don't have to be afraid any more. There are no Nazis in your life."

And yet there I am, not so far away as you would imagine after all this time, there in the classroom with that kind teacher. She was waiting for me to speak, and I stared at my drawing. She tucked her hand into mine and we sat on the lower steps of a small stage in the classroom. Slowly, my voice came to me. "When the bombs fell, the sky became black, and I was scared that the planes would shoot at me." Outside, snowflakes drifted down and stuck to the tree branches. That day the sky was not black; it was quiet and white, all white.

I remember another time when my class went into a different room filled with rows of wooden benches. A tall young man, handsome and slim like my brother Sam, but just a little older, walked quietly into the room. He wore a black suit with a white collar around his neck, and, standing straight up, led us in prayer and talked about the meaning of Easter, a holiday I had not heard of until then. I had never experienced this kind of ceremony in the few times I went to synagogue. Somebody, maybe a teacher, explained to me later that the man was a priest, and that I was attending a Catholic school. Despite the confusion that raced through my mind, I felt comfortable in his presence and in that room, the school's chapel. I hadn't been in a house of prayer since Leo's bar mitzvah in October 1941.

But, when the priest began to make a certain sign to mark the prayer's end, I realized he was turning his movement into a cross. I suddenly stopped midway, having followed the priest's hand movements, becoming aware of what I was doing, saying to myself, I don't belong here. I'm Jewish! I knew what the cross meant. I could still remember the huge one hanging outside that beautiful church in Abbeville on that fateful day in May 1940 when Hitler commanded his forces to halt their ferocious fire. I was ashamed and thought what Papa would have said if he saw me praying in a chapel. The student next to me seemed confused when he saw my right hand falling to the side before I completed the sign.

The Swiss released Mama from the displaced persons camp in August 1943 and she went to live with Rachel, her mother, whom she hadn't seen but once since spending her teenage years at the orphanage. Nacha was now forty years old. How did that encounter go after twenty-five years of separation? Did they greet each other with kisses and hugs? Was there anger in Mother's face? Was there sadness in her mother's face? Did they talk about it at all, or were they simply glad to be together? My mother cheated me out of asking these questions because I didn't know until a decade later why she was abandoned. Perhaps she wouldn't have told me even had I known. She didn't like to remember some things.

On my seventh birthday, my foster parents put me on a train to visit Mama in Zürich. I looked forward to seeing her, ready to give her a big smile, but I was overwhelmed by a cold feeling when I approached my mother waiting for me on the platform.

She didn't even attempt a smile, nor talk much on the way to her mother's apartment by trolley, except ask questions and reply to mine. She just stared out the window, a blank stare as if no houses existed, there were no trees to look at, no people on the street.

I don't know how long it took, but finally she turned to me and cupped my hand into hers. "Happy birthday, my darling child," she said softly, kissing me on the cheek. The warmth of her hand made me feel better.

"Siest gut aus, mein schein yingl," she told me. You look good, my handsome little boy. "Still standing in front of the mirror combing your hair?" She smiled, and so did I, both of us flashing back to the time in Nice when I stood before the mirror combing my hair just the right way, trying to impress my curly-haired sweetheart.

"How is Leo?" I asked, wondering why he wasn't here to greet me.

"You'll see Leo when he gets off from school," Mama told me. "He's still living with a family, a very nice family. They have been so good to him, and their son Bernhard and Leo have become such good friends."

"And what about Papa, is he at work?"

"Papa is in a camp like we were. But he's doing fine. I get letters from him. He said he hopes to see us soon. Sam is very happy living in Lisbon."

We got off at the stop where my grandmother lived and walked up five flights of stairs to get to her apartment. When Grandmother opened the door, I was hit by a musty smell so thick I had to hold in my breath for fear of choking. Grandmother kissed me weakly on the cheek, her lips as cold as ice, in stark contrast to the steam hissing from the apartment's radiators. She was only in her early sixties, but her hunched shoulders and a face as rough as sandpaper made her look much older.

I heard someone moan in another room. Mama mentioned that I would get to see Abraham, whom she referred to as my grandfather. I walked into his room. He was lying in bed covered up to his neck with a thick army blanket, his long, pure-white beard carefully combed over it.

"He's dying," Mama explained to me. "You shouldn't see this," she added, whisking me out of his bedroom.

I didn't spend much time with my grandmother as she was busy feeding Abraham and tending to his needs. The evening of my birthday, Mama and I went to see Leo at the home of the Lehrer's, the family he was living with, and had dinner with them. I was treated to a birthday cake.

I felt very welcome by the family and thought how lucky Leo was to have the Lehrer's as his foster parents. I warmed up to them quickly, and knowing what Mama was going through with Rachel and Abraham, they asked Mama whether I could stay with them overnight to spend more time with Leo, who weeks before celebrated his fifteenth birthday. I was thrilled because I wanted to tell Leo something that I did not want Mama to know: David had attacked me.

During summer 1943, while living with my foster family, I had played with a small ceramic toy, perhaps a toy soldier—I don't remember—that belonged to David. When I replaced the toy, I made the mistake of placing it close to the edge of his display case where he kept his other treasures. The toy teetered and fell to the floor, breaking into small pieces. When David discovered the ruined toy, he flew into a rage. He tossed me onto a bed and held me there. In an instant, he tore off my clothes and plunged a bicycle pump into my behind, pumping over and over. I was stunned, shocked, unable even to let out a scream. I was in unbearable pain. Only when darkness closed in on me was I freed from this terror.

The next thing I knew I was taking a bath, my shame growing as David's parents stood over my naked body. They sweet-talked me and plied me with fried eggs and hash browns, as if that could undo what their son had done. It would not be the last time their son would lash out. He took delight in stripping me and tying me to a chair. He would lock me in the closet.

I would have confided to Mama if I felt she didn't want me to go back to St. Gallen. But, she had made no effort for me to stay with her, and, seeing the strain she was under, and having misgivings about changing school and making new friends, I thought I would be better off in St. Gallen.

I returned after only one day with my mother, disappointed that she didn't even ask me to live with her. She must have had a lot on her mind, and probably needed to care for herself first, to regroup after more than three years on the run and twice being a prisoner. I never held that rejection against her. She had been through too much.

I wondered later what she felt for her feeble old stepfather. Was she anxious to see him die? Mama had too much kindness for that to have crossed her mind, and I'm sure she forgave my grandmother and simply was grateful to live in Switzerland. I wished she had told me the truth about why she didn't accompany her mother and her mother's new husband to Switzerland, but she chose to remain silent. In many ways, I was no different. I, too, never told her about David's abuses to me.

Chapter 25

THE FINAL STEP

In November 1943, the Swiss finally released Papa from Büren, thirteen months after our escape from France. What I learned later is that during much of my parents' imprisonment, beginning in October 1942, World War II was raging from North Africa to Russia.

Field Marshall Bernard Montgomery and his British forces won crucial control of Egypt's vast desert El Alamein, handing Germany's Field Marshal Rommel a major defeat that set the stage for the eventual demise of Hitler and the final curtain on his warped dream of ruling the world for the "next one thousand years." The battle began 23 October and ended 5 November.

In Russia, the Battle of Stalingrad saw German and Soviet units engaged in fierce urban fighting for control of that city. By November, the Russian armies surrounded the Germans, and forced the exhausted, half-frozen units to surrender on 31 January 1943. Nearly 2 million Russian and German soldiers were killed in that six-month battle.

Throughout the coming months the Nazis continued to suffer more devastating defeats. In Italy, American and British forces moved steadily forward through Sicily, Salerno, and Cassino, 75 miles south of Rome, where some of the most brutal fighting of World War II took place. Mussolini had been toppled from power, and the new Italian government declared war on Germany, ending the alliance between those two nations.

On the eastern front, Soviet troops slowly pushed the Germans back into Poland.

But it was El Alamein and Stalingrad that became the turning points of the war, with the Germans mostly in retreat thereafter until their surrender in 1945.

Sensing Germany's ultimate defeat, the Swiss government, in August 1943, began releasing imprisoned Jews from the displaced persons camps. Would Mama and Papa have ever been released if Switzerland believed Germany would win the war? Hitler gave that answer: "The Jews must...disappear from Europe...They'll also have to clear out of Switzerland...We cannot allow them to retain bases of withdrawal at our doors."

On Christmas Eve 1943, far different from 1941, snow fell on St. Gallen as predictably as the sun rises each day. My Catholic schoolteacher took me on a hike to a country church for midnight mass outside of town. The church was no bigger than a one-room schoolhouse and seemed separated from the rest of the world in a field with nothing around to disturb its serenity. The lone white steeple, the surroundings, and the falling snow made the setting a perfect picture for a Christmas card. We were outdoors with a small group of carolers who were singing along with the music piped out from the church. I stood in awe of this tiny building, which was framed by a black sky that twinkled with a million stars. I was seized by the contentment a child feels when tucked into bed and kissed goodnight. The teacher held my hand as we sang *Silent Night*.

I was reunited with my parents in Zürich in February 1944, more than a year after leaving them. I wasn't looking forward to leaving St. Gallen and making yet another change. I enjoyed the school, my friends, and the freedom to roam around. I liked gazing out my back window watching the cows graze in the pasture beyond the electric fence. And I wanted to make another sunflower grow. I felt safe with my temporary parents because David wasn't around anymore; he simply vanished one day. I also wondered how warmly Mama would welcome me, now burdened by caring for her mother after her stepfather had died.

Cramped in a two-bedroom apartment with my parents and grandmother wasn't easy. Papa, Leo, and I slept in the larger room. Mama shared the other room with grandmother. Our room, which served as a living room during the day, was dark and dreary with only one attic window. I would climb up to sit on its wide windowsill and look down five floors below to watch the children play in the street. I begged Mama to let me join them. She turned me down. "Nein!" she repeated harshly. I hated her at that moment. At times like this, I felt that I would never again regain my childhood that had been so abruptly interrupted by Hitler, that Mama would never let me, and I resented her for it.

Papa had found a job as a diamond cutter, and I was enrolled in the second grade at a public school about 2 miles from my grandmother's house. Mama got along well with her mother, but Papa didn't. They argued about the rent and the fact that he didn't want to contribute his share, Rachel suspecting he was squandering his paycheck.

Papa's past habits led to his reputation as a gambling addict. Obviously, Mama had let grandmother know about his loose behavior. Papa's relationship with his mother-in-law grew so strained that I once overheard grandmother pleading with Mama to leave him. Grandmother was not openly friendly or affectionate; she rarely kissed or hugged me and gave me few presents. It seemed that she wanted to remain alone with Mama, probably to compensate for their many years apart.

My happiest times were spent in school and with my friends, just as they were in St. Gallen. I was the best reader in class, which was a skill judged more on speed than comprehension. There were times I got into trouble and my teacher, Ms. Stöckli, would call me to her desk. Under her staring eyes and the I'm-glad-it's-not-me grins of my classmates, I had to walk what seemed a mile from the last row of seats to her desk, and then stick out my thumb for a swift, vicious slap of her ruler—almost always because of talking in class. Other times I played hooky from school and sometimes getting caught and suffering a spanking from Papa. I took other risks as well when skipping school, like walking on the narrow edge of a nearby bridge with a classmate.

Papa and I attended synagogue regularly on the Sabbath. An old man who children thought to be over a hundred years old held my interest there. He wore a black robe and a black felt hat with a wide brim. A bit stooped, he stood up to pray. He rarely dozed off, as Papa did frequently, when the rabbi delivered his sermon. I looked forward to the Sabbath just to see whether the old man would show up. One day, in late 1944, he didn't.

I loved playing soccer, which in Switzerland is called fussball, German for football, and accompanied my best friend and his father to professional games. I listened avidly to the games on radio and was able to mimic almost blow-by-blow the cadence of the animated broadcasters, fluctuating my voice to match the ecstasy of a goal scored by the home team or the mournful tone of defeat. Almost every Sunday that we went to the café with Mama's cousins, I was asked to emulate a game and never balked at the opportunity to perform.

Another favorite family activity was strolling down Zürich's main avenue, Banhofstrasse, and watching passersby promenade arm-in-arm or sit at outside coffee houses. One time I brushed shoulders with a lean German officer, dressed in a stark gray uniform, high black boots and a fancy visor cap. What was he doing here? Maybe taking a break from the war? Or, as the world later discovered in the 1990s, he could have been secretly doing business with the Swiss banks. These banks had financed Germany's war production, accepting as payments deposits of gold confiscated from Jews, including the millions of gold-plated teeth gruesomely extracted from the bodies in the killing camps.

The Allies, including the US Army, Navy, and Army-Air Forces, broke through the German defenses in Italy in May 1944, about the same time that Sam Katz and his two sons were released from the Büren slave-labor camp where Papa had been held. On 4 June the US Army 5th Regiment entered Rome. And on 6 June 1944, the D-Day invasion began that would free France and seal Hitler's fate.

Roughly 2,700 ships equipped with landing crafts carried 176,000 Allied soldiers from the shores of Great Britain across the choppy English Channel. Led by American soldiers, the troops stormed the beaches of northern France in the Normandy region. They landed a few miles south of the coastline where four years before the ferocious German bombardments had almost killed us. The Allies used the beaches to unload more combat soldiers and supplies. More than one million troops reached France within that month and wrested control of the country from the Nazis.

As the fighting raged in northern France, Leo and I were sent to a Jewish summer camp located in the northern Alps of

Switzerland near the town of Schaffhausen. One afternoon we went hiking with a small group from camp. We trudged a few miles through through fields and meadows, fighting off the bees and prickly underbrush. When we reached the shore of Lake Constance, the director pointed to what he said was an installation where the Nazis killed Jewish people. He directed our attention toward the southern border of Germany, to a town that I would learn was Friedrichshafen, the site of a subcamp to the Dachau concentration camp.

I gazed at the shimmering blue lake, a slight breeze rippling the waters. I believed death occurred only in dark and forbidding places, not at a scenic place where people vacationed. Jewish prisoners across the border were forced into labor, manufacturing weapons and rebuilding roads and bridges after the Allies' bombardment of the town and the Nazi armament factories in April 1944. All that had taken place at this lovely site. It was difficult to understand.

On 15 August 1944, nearly 100,000 British and Canadian troops tore through German lines in southern France and liberated Nice. Adolf Hitler described this as "the worst day of my life." Yet, many more worst days were on the way for Hitler: it was the beginning of his end. On 16 August, the Nazi leader ordered his forces to withdraw from southern France almost two years after we'd barely sidestepped the massive roundups. American forces liberated Paris a week later.

One day, fresh from our summer experience, Leo told me that US soldiers on leave from a battle were arriving at the Zürich train station. We rushed to see the hundreds of American GI's hanging around, relaxing on wooden benches, their cigars and cigarettes creating wisps of smoke lingering above their heads.

Clutching a slip of paper, I approached a soldier a few years older than Leo. The blond-haired man had a smooth, strong-featured face, its roundness magnified by a crew cut that barely covered his skull. His muscles protruded from his rolled-up shirt sleeves. I stretched my arm out as far as I could to hand him the ripped scrap on which Leo had written, "chewing gum, please." The young man reached into his duffle bag and pulled out a pack of Wrigley's gum—plus a Baby Ruth candy! "Here, kid," is all he said in a slow drawl, softly smiling. It was the first time I heard English spoken by an American and that alone was enough to send me home with a great story to tell my friends. I just wished that Sam was around to hear my story—which surprised me since I hadn't thought much about him, though I knew from his letters to us that he was safe in Lisbon.

Shortly after my encounter with the American soldier, we heard the best news we'd had in a very long time. The Allies crossed into Belgium and on 4 September 1944 liberated my birthplace, Antwerp. We were going home. We just had to wait for the war to end, and that would take another eight months. The German troops gasped their last breath as they were wedged between the advancing Allied troops from the west and the Russians from the east, and American and British units slashing through southern Europe towards Berlin.

I got all my news from reading the *Neue Züricher Zeitung*, Zürich's major daily newspaper. I devoured the articles, imagining myself marching through the towns and villages liberated by the American and British forces, jumping with joy at every German defeat. Franklin Delano Roosevelt was my hero. I remember pinning on the wall over my bed a newspaper photograph of Roosevelt seated at a desk, giving an ear-to-ear smile for the camera, with James Byrnes, one of his top war aides, leaning over the president's left shoulder. It came down from the wall when it turned yellow and the edges curled over Roosevelt's face, but not before he died April 1945. The news of his death devastated me, and I feared that without Roosevelt the Nazis would win the war.

But good news leaped off the news pages. That same month, the Red Army stampeded into Berlin, driving Adolf Hitler to his heavily encased bunker below the Reich Chancellery, Nazi Germany's seat of government. On 30 April, the troops were only a few hundred yards from Hitler's hiding place. Having lost every chance of achieving his evil goals, Hitler shot himself that afternoon.

Following orders, SS bodyguards immediately set his body on fire with gasoline. Hitler's cowardly demise terminated this lunatic's rampaging and insane ambition to create a superior Aryan race of athletic-looking blond and blue-eyed Germans everywhere, and his dream of eliminating Europe's Jews.

On 7 May, Germany surrendered, and V-E Day, Victory in Europe Day, was declared on 8 May, five years after Belgium was invaded. Banhofstrasse in Zurich, Switzerland, where I performed my imaginary soccer broadcasts, was stretching at the seams to contain the tens of thousands of men, women, and children celebrating the Nazis defeat. I remember seeing a beautiful woman with jet-black hair and deep-red lipstick. She wore a white dress pinned in front and back, from neck to ankle with dozens of tiny national flags representing the victorious Allies. I tingled with excitement as I stared at her, and she returned my stare with what I now feel was probably a sensuous smile. I was eight, and girls were beginning to be important. Life was coming back to us all.

A few months after V-E Day, Papa made plans to go to America, once more phoning his New York relatives for help. They had helped Sam come to America in January 1946. Now, they would help us.

Chapter 26

COMING TO AMERICA

I had to warm up to the idea of coming to America. I had heard a lot about New York City, the skyscrapers scratching the clouds, money growing on trees, freedom to roam the streets without fearing arrest. I was certainly curious, but longed, I guess to see and hear the simple things I missed: the sound of the trains rolling by our home, walking the streets with my family, going to the park or zoo with my brothers.

I was fluent in French and German, but I doubted that I would ever be able to learn English. It sounded like Americans spoke with a hot potato in their mouths.

We flew—my first airplane ride—to Antwerp in February 1946, while my grandmother, a sad and lonely woman, remained in Switzerland. From one glance at a family portrait taken before our departure, her sadness is obvious, far different than the earlier photo of a determined, unsmiling young woman showing no remorse for what she was about to do to her teenage daughter. I've looked at that later photograph a thousand times, even enlarged it as a poster to show students.

Mama had begged her to accompany us, but she refused to leave her home. Grandmother died in 1948, and Mama grieved for her death—perhaps more for having come full circle, feeling she had abandoned her old mother as her then young mother had abandoned her. Maybe she grieved for both of them. Once in Antwerp our chores were to gather the belongings the landlord and old neighbor kept for us.

Fred Gross

Mama: After the war, we sent somebody to this neighbor; he should bring us back the luggage. The neighbor said, 'I haven't got it. The Germans took it.' It wasn't the truth. The good stuff was robbed, and when we came back to Antwerp after the war, the landlord gave us back most of the furniture he stored in a warehouse. We sold it.

What about the photographs?

Mama: We left them behind in the apartment, but the landlord kept it for us.

She couldn't know the conditions of Nazi rule while we were gone. Perhaps our neighbor did tell the truth. Failing to meet their quota to deport 20,000 Belgian Jews by the end of August 1942, the Gestapo raided Jewish residences. The Germans may have barged into our apartment searching for us and interrogated the other tenants as to our whereabouts. The neighbor might indeed have handed over our possessions out of fear.

We stayed for two months in Antwerp in a hotel off the Keyserlei (the main boulevard) before boarding a ship for America. We couldn't even enter the old apartment. It had been rented. When I returned, I had expected to see a ruined city, crumbled buildings everywhere, and empty streets. Instead, people walked almost shoulder-to-shoulder to work or to shop or to go out to lunch. Cars and trucks jammed the streets as drivers honked impatiently. I wondered how things could be so normal after my terrible ordeal—it was like time stood still and for all the non-Jews everything was just as it was.

One image raised my eyebrows: a scrawny, shaggy young garbage collector with scruffy blond hair. The man wore striped prison garb with one mark that distinguished him from other jailed inmates. Three huge letters were painted haphazardly in black on his shirt: POW. He was a Nazi soldier taken prisoner by the Belgians and working detail on a garbage truck. I just stared, and he responded with a cocky laugh as he hopped on the back of the moving sanitation truck to disappear amid the traffic.

The street photographer, a fixture from pre-war days, was still there and we allowed her to take pictures of us just days before we boarded the USS James W. Johnson. It was a creaky mass of a ship, one of nearly 3,000 that shipbuilders assembled quickly to transport war supplies. President Roosevelt had admiringly dubbed these Liberty Ships as the Ugly Ducklings. In late March 1946, the USS Johnson would begin its 3,000-mile journey across the Atlantic with us on board.

Soon after we were assigned cabins, a lieutenant aboard the ship invited our family to the captain's quarters to raise a glass of cognac to toast our voyage to America. When the lieutenant jokingly extended a drink to me, Mama's arm brushed by me to grab the glass of cognac. The captain, an officer of the US Merchant Marines, took a liking to us, gauging by his gesture and tone of voice, not by his words—we couldn't understand English. When his voice lilted to a question, we nodded our heads. The lieutenant slowly drifted off as he emptied the bottle. Soon, I was on deck watching sailors lifting a limp, drunken officer onto a stretcher, and slowly hoisting the lieutenant over the rail and lowering him by rope to the pier and a waiting ambulance.

Several hours later, the ship left the Antwerp harbor, heading for the English Channel to cross the Atlantic Ocean. The USS Johnson passed by a row of sunken war ships littering the shallow water, their tops protruding as if gasping for air. From our vessel's deck, I saw small towns on the river's edge, their little white and brown-trimmed houses and corrugated red tiled roofs, flowerpots brimming with reds, yellows, whites, and greens. It was a picture-postcard that magically came to life. For most of our three weeks at sea, we traveled through violent storms as the *USS Johnson* was hurled about like a toy boat caught in a current manufactured in the bathtub by a child's splash.

Often, we were scared the ship would capsize as it tilted dangerously close to the raging waters, flinging open doors, and sending dishes, tables, and chairs crashing. I had fun leaning one way to keep my balance when the vessel tipped the other way. And I became friendly with a twenty-year-old sailor who worked in the suffocating heat of the engine room. As we approached the United States, he showed me the three-cylinder steam engine hissing and clanking, and talked to me. About what, I do not know. But his voice was serious, his face solemn. He pointed to the intricately embroidered Swiss skullcap I was wearing as a yarmulke, and after touching it with one hand and pointing to himself with the other, I knew that he wanted it. In exchange, he gave me his Merchant Marine knife. I still treasure the knife.

On 16 April 1946, the *USS Johnson* arrived under an umbrella of blue sky at the US Naval Base in Norfolk, Virginia, docking at a pier surrounded by a huge aircraft carrier and destroyers. No fanfare, no Statue of Liberty to greet us. But I felt welcomed by the military's quiet display of power. Nobody could harm me now.

While my parents were processed by immigration officials who boarded the ship, I stood with Leo at the stern looking down at the pier, my concentration rooted to the stark gray cement, until I was distracted by the noise of sailors playing dice. One tall and handsome gambler, with a flowing handlebar moustache, held a fistful of dollars. Crouching like a baseball catcher, he rolled the dice and his buddies cheered.

Then Mama, Papa, Leo, and I descended the gangplank to hop into a jeep that took us to the train depot. As we pulled away, I glanced back at the *USS James W. Johnson*, wondering at its destiny. At the conclusion of my personal odyssey, I learned that the ship was built in California, was launched into action 30 December 1943, and served as a cargo vessel throughout the war, ferrying airplanes, tanks, jeeps, and weapons to American troops fighting in the Pacific against Japan and in Europe against Germany. The ship was put into the reserve fleet after the war and scrapped in January 1971.

I had no idea when we arrived later in the city of Norfolk that Virginia practiced discrimination against another race—blacks—as did much of the country prior to the civil rights movement. It took some time before I fully understood how my new homeland had its own version of some of what we had experienced in World War II. African-Americans attended separate schools from whites, were refused service at hotels and restaurants, and were relegated to the back seats of public buses.

We had to wait awhile to board the train to New York, where we would be united after a four-year absence with our brother Sam, who had arrived from Portugal in January. After about a half-hour wait on a bench outside the station, I went to the restroom where I saw a little old man, probably more than seventy years old, wearing a crumpled brown hat, brown tweed jacket, and baggy brown pants. When we made eye contact, his sweet smile creased his weather-beaten face. He had skin darker than I had ever seen. Exiting together, I saw Leo talking with a blond, crew-cut young man wearing trousers tightened at the cuffs.

"What's the matter?" I asked my brother in German.

"He told me you shouldn't have gone in there," Leo replied.

"Why not?"

Leo pointed to the restroom sign. It read, "Colored Men Only."

CONCLUSION

So the journey is over...or is it? Yes, that veil of forgetfulness that dimmed my memories has been partially lifted. Still, there remains one question: Am I truly a Holocaust survivor?

Our family wasn't deported to Auschwitz as thousands in Camp Gurs had been.

We were not huddled inside the apartment when the French police stormed into our hotel in Nice before dawn and smashed down our door. No, we had gone, escaped.

We had not been caught when we were traveling with Uncle Emil.

The French police missed snatching us along our escape route to Switzerland.

We were not among the panic-stricken refugees the Swiss guards dragged across the French border into the waiting clutches of the French collaborators.

If we had remained interned in Gurs or did not leave our Nice hotel during the roundups, if my parents' passports were discovered to be forgeries, if my grandmother had not lived in Switzerland, death was as certain as day turning into night.

Sadly, three of Father's siblings did not make it. Aunt Malie, a kindergarten teacher, her husband, and a daughter were never heard from again. Another daughter, Hilde, did survive. Hilde fled Germany in 1935 to escape Hitler's purge of communists, living in exile in Poland and Czechoslovakia, then fleeing to France and from there to Mexico. Hilde settled briefly in the United States before departing for communist East Germany, where she became editor of a stylish, cultural magazine, *Das Magazin*. Yet despite her high status, Hilde could not step out of the long dark shadow cast by the destruction of her family. The only comfort she found was in her work and in the warmth of her colleagues, who described her as "often sad and lonely." They remember her saying to them on her first day as editor, "You are now my family."

Uncle Naftalie, and his wife lived in Krakow, Poland where he served as cantor in a synagogue. They were never heard of again.

Uncle Hermann owned a tobacco shop in Frankfurt before 1939. He fled to France with his wife and their two children at the dawn of the Second World War, never imagining this land of liberty stoked by the French Revolution would march in step with Hitler to murder its Jewish population. Hermann and his wife were deported from France on 12 July 1943 to Auschwitz, never to return. The French police captured them merely steps away from crossing into Italy. Their son survived and the daughter committed suicide in 1986, no doubt haunted for decades by the specter of the war's atrocities, and the destruction of her family.

They are all only alive through memories.

Not once did Papa talk to me about his two brothers and sister. I never saw Papa cry over his missing siblings, but I remember a deep sobbing coming from him when his brother Salomon died of natural causes in Holland in 1952. Salomon, the black sheep of the family, left home as a teenager to live in Holland where he married a Gentile woman, a marriage described as "the height of filial disrespect." Salomon evaded the Nazi roundups in which 75 percent of the Dutch-Jewish population of 140,000 perished. It is not known how Salomon survived, or if he rode on his wife's Christianity to save his life.

And what about Julius Kurz, the distant cousin who notified us of the imminent raid on our hotel in Nice? He disappeared forever, too. The police found him hiding in his apartment and loaded him onto a freight train bound for Auschwitz. He saved us, but he couldn't save himself. He was deported 4 September 1942.

And I missed an opportunity to be with my father's twin, my Uncle Emil who escorted us to the edge of Switzerland, when I visited Leo in Paris in 1961. Papa instructed me to see my uncle. "You must see him," Papa implored, the words still ringing in my ear. He was very angry when I later told him that I didn't. Why didn't he tell me Emil had helped us dodge the roundups to escape into Switzerland? I was older when we escaped, but I didn't remember. Had I known I would have crawled the whole way from Paris to Strasbourg to see him, to thank him. He died of heart failure in 1964.

Aunt Hedwig returned to Paris after the war and died there in 1976.

Cigarettes silenced Papa in 1973, the memories of the war buried with him. Mama lived until 1989, leaving behind her memories to fill a void in my life, memories that lifted, to some extent, the veil that had kept me an outsider to my own story.

My brother Leo, my close friend, my protector, passed away in 2003 at the age of seventy-four. He sustained me through those terrible times, held me up when my spirits failed me, taught me how to ride a bicycle, a talent akin to a sixteen-year-old driving a car. Sam, the courageous brother who escaped from the Gurs concentration camp and returned to save our lives, celebrated his eighty-sixth birthday in December 2009.

And what of me? I feel lucky to be alive. If I had failed to take that final step to freedom, there would be no Adam, Marc, Josh, and Jonathan, my sons, and Haley, Dylan, Ashley, my grandchildren.

There are some special people to thank for that—the dozens of Righteous Gentiles who were there for us at every step of the journey. The French farmer in Dax; the mayor from Orin who helped rescue us from the Gurs camp; the two Italian consuls at Hôtel Continental who befriended us even though their country was Hitler's ally; Papa's Catholic friend who hid us in his home during the August–September 1942 roundups in Nice; the Portuguese consul in Pau who disobeyed an order to arrest Sam; and the Catholic nuns from Grenoble, who engineered our escape to Switzerland.

Today, I take great comfort in teaching students about the Holocaust and in sharing with them my childhood experiences. A shake of the head in disbelief, a sigh of anguish, a long silence with hardly a stir, and those searching eyes are the signs of understanding and compassion that bring purpose and satisfaction to my life. Rarely have these audiences failed me—and I won't fail them. I feel that if I have made a difference for one person, if I have taught even one person to be more human, to realize how precious and fragile, how irreplaceable humans and families are, I have fulfilled my role as a teacher and a survivor, and as a Jew.

A BIBLIOGRAPHIC NOTE

I used many sources in an effort to give a historical perspective to my story. It was important to demonstrate the way the German invasion into Belgium and France, and Vichy government policies and directives influenced the decisions we made throughout our flight. However, I decided not to include footnotes because I believed that these would detract from the drama and narrative flow of the book. The sources included books, documents and reports, newspaper articles, and reputable Holocaust online sites. Of these sources, Martin Gilbert's *The Second World War* and Robert Leckie's *Delivered From Evil* helped provide the historical setting for my family's flight from Belgium to France. Michael Marrus and Robert Paxon's *Vichy France and the Jews,* Serge Klarsfeld's *Le Calendrier,* and Susan Zuccotti's *The Holocaust, The French, and the Jews,* were penetrating books that informed me on the reasons we had to escape numerous times, seconds from being grasped by the Nazi collaborators. The other sources listed below also helped add substance and verification to our grueling wanderings.

Bibliography

Belgian Ministry of Foreign Affairs. *Belgium: The Official Account of What happened, 1939–1940.* New York: Didier Publishers, 1942.

Ben-Sasson, H. H. *A History of the Jewish People.* Cambridge: Harvard University Press, 1976.

Carse, Robert. *Dunkirk—1940: The rescue That Saved a Nation—and the Courage That Saved the World.* Englewood Cliffs NJ: Prentice-Hall, Inc., 1970.

Dawidowicz, Lucy S. *The War Against the Jews, 1933–1945.* New York: Bantam Books 1975.

Fittko, Lisa. *Escape through the Pyrenees.* Evanston IL: Northwestern University Press, 1985.

Fralon, José-Alain. *A Good Man in Evil Times: The Story of Aristides De Sousa Mendes – The Man who Saved the Lives of Countless Refugees in World War II.* New York: Carroll and Graf Publishers, Inc., 1998.

Gilbert, Martin. *The Holocaust, A History of the Jews of Europe During the Second World War.* New York: Henry Holt and Company, LLC, 1985.

———. *The Second World War: Revised Edition.* New York: Henry Holt and Company, 1989.

Gushee, David P. *The Righteous Gentiles of the Holocaust: A Christian Interpretation.* Minneapolis: Fortress Press, 1994.

Klarsfeld, Serge. *Le Calendrier: De la Persécution des Juifs en France, 1940–1944.* Paris: The Beate Klarsfeld Foundation, 1993.

Laharie, Claude. *Le Camp de Gurs, 1939-1945: Un Aspect Méconnu de L'histoire de Vichy.* Biarritz: J&D Editions, 1993.

Laquer, Walter. *The Holocaust Encyclopedia.* New Haven: Yale University Press, 2001.

LeBor, Adam. *Hitler's Secret Bankers: The Myth of Swiss Neutrality during the Holocaust.* Secaucus NJ: Carol Publishing Group, 1997.

Leckie, Robert. *Delivered From Evil: The Saga of World War II.* New York: Harper Perennial, 1987.

Marino, Andy. *A Quiet American: The Secret War of Varian Fry.* New York: St. Martin's Griffin, 2000.

Marrus, Michael R., and Robert O. Paxton, *Vichy France and the Jews,* New York: Schocken Books, 1983

Miller, Francis Trevelyan. *History of World War II: Armed Sevices Memorial Edition,* Philadelphia: Universal Book and Bible House,1945.

Monneray, Henri. *La Persecution des Juifs en France et Dans les Autres Pays de L'Ouest* Presentée par la France à Nuremburg. Paris: Centre de Documentation Juive Contemporaine, 1947.

Poliakov, Leon, and Jacques Sabille. *Jews under the Italian Occupation.* Paris: Centre de Documentation Juive Contemporaine,1954.

Poznanski, Renée. *Jews in France during World War II.* Hanover and London: University Press of New England, 1997.

Ryan, Donna F. *The Holocaust & the Jews of Marseille: The Enforcement of Anti-Semitic Policies in Vichy France.* Urbana and Chicago: Board of Trustees of the University of Illinois, 1996.

Schmidt, Ephraim. *Geschiedenis van de Joden in Antwerpen.* Antwerpen/Rotterdam: Uitgeverij C. De Vries-Brouwers B. V. B. A., 1963.

Zaretsky, Robert. *Nîmes at War: Religion, Politics, and Public Opinion in the Gard, 1938-1944.* University Park: Pennsylvania State University Press, 1995.

Zuccotti, Susan. *The Holocaust, the French, and the Jews.* New York: BasicBooks, 1993.

Plaut, W. Gunther, and David E. S. Stein, eds. *The Torah: A Modern Commentary.* Revised edition. New York: Union for Reform Judaism, 2005.

INDEX

Index

National Socialist Workers' Party,
55
Neue Züricher Zeitung, 187
New York City, United States,
190
Nice, France; arrival in, 118;
beach at, 123; civil rights
granted to Jews in, 119;
clothing in, 118; founding of,
119; Gross, S., escapes to
Portugal, 134; Gross, S., leaves
for Vichy from, 132; Gross, S.,
return to, 132; Italian
jurisdiction of, 117; Italians
protect Jews in, 126–127;
Italy occupies, 70; Jews and,
119, 139; Kurz, C., fleeing,
136; liberation of, 186; luxury
in, 118; photos from, 123;
Promenades des Anglais in,
123–124; Statute of, 119;
Vichy government start
roundups, 132
Night of Broken Glass, 50, 92
nightmares, 174–175
Norfolk, Virginia, 193;
immigration officials in, 193–
194
Nuremberg Law, 113

Oloron-Sainte-Marie, France, 91;
arrival in, 100–101; Gestapo
in, 101
Orin, France, 91; castle in, 99–
100; evacuation of, 100;
Gross, S., arrival in, 89

Pabianice, Poland, 29; ghetto in,
126
Palais de la Méditerranée, 124
Paris, France: arrival in, 62;

bombing of, 68; bonfires of
government documents in,
63; curfew in, 72; declared as
open city, 71; Germans
march into, 72; Hitler's visit
to, 74–75; liberation of, 186;
panic in, 62; train for, 60–61
Paris-Plage, France, 37, 58
passeur. *See* smuggler
Passover, 16–17
passports, forged, 150
Pau, France, 78; Boulevard des
Pyrénées in, 79; Place Royale
in, 79; school in, 79–80
payes, 48
Pétain, Henri Philippe, 73, 75,
126
*Pétain's Crime: The Complete Story
of French Collaboration in the
Hollocaust* (Webster), 168
Petit Saleve, 159
planes, 173–174. *See also*
Luftwaffe; Stukas; first ride in,
190; nightmares of crashing,
174–175
pogroms, 30, 46
Poland. *See also specific cities in
Poland*; birthplace of Feivel,
45; German invasion of, 4,
65; ghettos liquidated in, 134
Police D'Etat, 114
Portugal, 68. *See also specific cities
in Portugal*; entry visa, 111;
Gross, S., acquiring visa to,
131, 133; proof of destination
to another country required
by, 102
Prague, Czechoslovakia, 14
Putsch, 55–56
Pyrénées Mountains, 78